The
Giveaway
God

The Giveaway God

Ecumenical Bible Studies on Divine Generosity

John Bluck

WCC Publications, Geneva

Cover design: Rob Lucas
Cover photo: Jessica Bluck

ISBN 2-8254-1347-X

No. 93 in the Risk Book Series

Printed in Switzerland

Contents

Introduction

I joined the World Council of Churches staff back in 1977, having trained as a priest and an ecumenical journalist, and thinking I knew something about Bible study. Very quickly, I found I knew very little. In fact, I had to start all over again.

Because studying scripture cross-culturally, and trying to hold together the radically diverse ways that different Christian traditions see the same text, meant I could never again open the Bible complacently. I learnt to respect the volatility of scripture and its power to build community on bare ground.

Three decades on from serving that ecumenical apprenticeship, I am still trying to handle the Bible with the care and respect I learnt from sitting and listening in small groups gathered from every church and culture under God.

These days, I work in a local, denominational setting, but I still try to read and preach the Bible through the eyes of the worldwide church. And people seem to respond. If anything, the local hunger to let texts speak globally is stronger than ever. In that way, the ecumenical movement still thrives, hard though that may be to recognize at times.

The list of mentors and motivators for my own ecumenical journey is very long. When I come to write it out one day, Jan Kok will have to appear among the first for reasons he would be the last to know. Like his own mentor, W.A. Visser 't Hooft, he is still a good Dutch Calvinist underneath all the experience he's gained from being the World Council's publisher for these last three decades. With a consistency that's hard to match in a council and a movement that has changed so much, Jan has held to the centrality of scripture and promoted its exploration with great professionalism and skill. I had never met a serious religious publisher before I met Jan, though I've met dozens since. I was lucky to start with the best. Ecumenically, we were an unlikely combination. Dutch Calvinist and New Zealand Anglican. But we have walked some good miles together. I am proud to dedicate this book to him.

JOHN BLUCK

PART ONE
Old Stories Made New

Girls can do anything (boys too)

> As Jesus travels about, teaching and healing, he is moved to pity by the crowds who seem to him to be like sheep without a shepherd, harassed and helpless. He tells his disciples that the harvest is heavy and more labourers are needed. (Matt. 9:35ff.)

This is not a good time to be a sheep in New Zealand. Especially if you're young, dead and frozen and on your way to the American market. You won't fetch the price you deserve. What's more, you'll have to contend with a genetically modified and cloned cousin called Dolly who is alive and well and growing old at three times the normal rate.

It's a very difficult and confusing time to be a sheep. No one would blame you for feeling harassed and helpless.

And this is not a good time to be a plant. Global warming is altering the seasons and messing up your time clock. It's midwinter yet still warm enough to have you bursting into blossom. And even if you manage to escape dangerous sprays and marauding insects, all the genetic modification going on is enough to give any self-respecting crop an identity crisis.

If I were writing a gospel today, I wouldn't talk about plants or sheep, or any kind of livestock for that matter, especially if I lived in Europe. But Jesus talks a lot about sheep and plants, as symbols of the church's work, linking them together in some verses in Matthew. That's odd, because sheep and plants had little in common in the first century. Sheep needed a great deal of looking after and plants needed hardly any: you sowed the seeds and simply watched them grow to harvest. No spraying, no irrigation, not even any weeding, according to a later parable. God took care of plants and brought them to harvest.

So here you have two contrasting images of the church. One says that you need to get busy seeking out, caring, serving, healing people in need. The other says that it doesn't all depend on you: God will provide and all manner of things shall be well.

We hear plenty about the first face of the church. We know all about being harassed and helpless sheep. The hymn-books are full of songs about them. Jesus looks at this powerless, despairing part of our experience and confronts it with compassion, which could also be translated as gut reaction. He addresses our despair about the flock and says it doesn't have to be this way. The sick can be healed. The dead can be raised. The demons can be beaten. The despairing can hope and trust again.

And, what's more, it doesn't all depend on Jesus doing the work of restoration and liberation. He empowers us to do it ourselves: everything I can do, you can do as well, if not better. The gospel is very clear about this. There's a precise parallel between the things that Jesus does for us and the things that he delegates to others, first the twelve apostles and eventually ourselves. I can bring hope. So can you. I can serve others. So can you. I can be a channel of God's healing power. So can you.

And you don't have to be someone specially gifted, let alone very religious and endowed with great faith. Not according to the gospel. The list of disciples is about as ordinary a catalogue of local people from down the road and round the corner as you could find. There's Peter the fisherman. They also call him Simon, and a few other names as well, I'll bet. And his brother Andrew; they don't make such a fuss about him, but I think he's a nicer fellow. And James; of course, he's Zebedee's boy, remember, a chip off the old block, more's the pity, the old man didn't amount to anything, and his brother John – I was never sure about him. And then Matthew was roped in. Yes, the tax collector fellow who is probably a crook. He always was a shady character. How could he do a job like that? Ripping off his own people. What was Jesus thinking of to pick him, to say nothing of the rest of that motley lot?

We know nothing much about this startling twelve, except that they were local nobodies, from nowhere, going nowhere. That's how it was. You can imagine how people talked about them. Yet this unlikely team was entrusted with the task of turning the world around. He gave them a confidence to take on anything. So why were they able to be so effective? It certainly wasn't because of their origins or education or superior resources. They didn't even have any computer skills. What equipped these helpless sheep to start so boldly, from right where they were, and achieve so much?

Maybe their confidence came from understanding better than we do this imagery of harvest. Clearly, for them, it wasn't an invitation to sit back and leave the growing to God. They weren't at all passive. But somehow they must have trusted Jesus's promise of a world that really does rest in the palm of God's hand, of a history that God really does have under control, however mysteriously.

Robert Capon talks about a God who rides the bicycle of history with no hands, seeming to take the most amazing risks, employing the most outrageous and unsuitable characters, welding together impossible partnerships, letting bad things happen to good people and watching bad people get away with murder. It all looks very unfair to us, muddled at best.

But the image of the harvest is a way of looking at the world through God's eyes and not our own. It's God's energy that drives this ripening growth, God's timetable, God's economy, God's way of being present and alive. And Jesus is so confident that God is in control that he seems almost careless and cavalier. He chooses the most ridiculously inadequate bunch of people to start a church and launch an ecumenical movement, he sets them the most impossible task and later on tells them not to worry about it all. Be like the birds and the flowers. Live for today. Trust in miracles. This is harvest mentality. Relax. Be ready to be surprised by this overflowing crop that exceeds all expectations, upsets all measures.

It takes great faith to believe that. Most of us settle for a few scraps that fall from the table of this harvest feast. It takes great faith to see God at work in this way because so much of the work is done secretly, silently, in the darkness as well as in the bright light of day; over the long, long term, by people who don't wear religion on their sleeves.

If you're a marketer or a public relations consultant, then God would be a nightmare client. Because if Jesus is to be believed, God neither draws attention to self, nor demands copyright permission and control. God's love is profligate, extravagant, free of charge, made to be given away. And that is what the church is called to be like. We exist for those who haven't yet heard the message; our reason for being insiders is to serve the outsiders. We're the only organization in the world where the interests of the members come last, not first.

Is that sensible? Of course it's not. Will it safeguard success and growth for the church? Of course it won't. But if the image of the harvest is to be trusted, we don't have to worry about the future of the church, let alone the ecumenical movement. If we embrace this confidence Jesus offers, somehow take it in, under our skin, then we'll see that it's the future of the world, not the church, that really matters, the same world that God so loved that he sent Jesus to redeem it. That's our mission impossible; yet, at the same time, it's a mission that God already has under control. We'll go on singing, no doubt, about frail and trembling sheep, but let's sing even more about the harvest. That gives us a marvellous image of God's way of being in the world – silently, beautifully, consistently. Trust that to be true and we'll be able to face the future with all the confidence we need.

Outrageous agriculture

Jesus tells the parable of the sower who scatters seed on all sorts
of ground, hard and rocky, choked with thorns, but finally on
good soil where grain is produced thirty-, sixty-, a hundredfold.
(Matt. 13:1ff.)

Do you ever wonder why the church seems to be in
trouble today? Why the people who used to come, prefer to
sleep in and read the Sunday paper? There are no simple
answers, of course. The Sunday paper isn't that compelling.
So what's going on?

Some people are just plain impossible when it comes to
believing in anything outside themselves beyond the next
lottery draw. That's the way they've always been. And then
there are the ones who make a lot of noise about believing,
then fade away. Enthusiasts, full of sound and certainty, but
signifying nothing. What a lovely choir, they say on Sunday.
What a lovely church. You can count on me. But by Thurs-
day they've moved on to even lovelier things like house and
garden and golf and you don't see them again.

There's another more promising group who really are
committed to growing in faith and they do for a while, until
they are finally ground down by all the other competing
demands on their time and energy: difficult children, awk-
ward relatives, ill health, unemployment, Sunday shopping,
sporting obligations.

That's what's wrong with the church today. We simply
don't have enough people we can count on. If only we had
more of the right kind of people. So, as the 21st century
begins, we hire people called church growth consultants and
marketers to show us where we've gone wrong and how to
increase our market share. We need to listen to their advice,
but we shouldn't listen too closely, if the parable in chapter
13 of Matthew's gospel has anything to say.

It's pretty difficult to hear just what the reading is saying.
For a start, the parable of the sower and the seed, and the pre-
soaked and flavoured interpretation Matthew offers, seem to
be saying slightly different things and are written in two different styles. The parable focuses on different sorts of soil,
yet the interpretation seems to be more interested in different

sorts of seed. What's more, the parable is written, as it is in Mark's gospel, with a lot of flourishes – very thin soil, very hot sun – that set you up for later explanation, like clues in a detective novel. There are versions of this parable that don't have such additions. In the gospel of Thomas, for example, which never made it into the New Testament, this story is told very straightforwardly, without any of the allegory that later versions carry.

And we know from other parables that Jesus told these stories very simply, in order to shock and surprise us into a new way of thinking about God. He didn't go in for those elaborately complicated puzzles that theologians and the designers of crossword puzzles delight in, where everything is meant to point to something else and nothing is what it seems. Parables were made to be spoken to illiterate Galilean peasants, not clever middle-class people who know more about the Internet than they do about growing enough wheat to live on.

So what is the simple point of this simple story? I think it's a message designed to reassure a church that was just about as anxious as ours: a church that at the end of the first century had hardly begun, was up against a hostile Roman empire so strong that it could close the Christians down as easily as swatting a housefly, and a suspicious Jewish establishment that was even more hostile to the followers of this blaspheming pseudo-rabbi they had crucified forty years before.

The early church for which this gospel was written was even more twitchy than we are about our future. They had no cathedrals to reassure them about the durability of the faith. They were desperate to know why the resurrection promise that had so inspired them was already failing. You can't blame them for falling on this parable. So they called in the psychoanalysts, the theologians and the spin doctors of the day and used the story to explain their failure and ease their anxiety. Well, what can you expect from these sorts of people – the quickly burnt-off types, the shallow rooters, the easily choked. Such explanations don't fit the story Jesus told, but they did provide some blessed assurance at the time. And who are we, so nervous ourselves, to criticize that?

If there is one overwhelming point to this parable, it lies not in the different sorts of soil or seed, but simply in the deliberately ridiculous yield figure that Jesus claims for the seed that fell on the good soil, as high as a hundredfold. The average yield for a Palestinian farmer at that time was about sevenfold, tenfold if you were an expert farmer working the richest river flats. But a hundredfold? That's just silly, way beyond any human achievement, no matter how high your skills and staying power. And that's the first point of the parable, even though it comes at the end: a promise of God's assurance to a church anxious about its future, saying that it doesn't all depend on us. The kingdom or, to use a translation that would have made more sense to the people of Palestine living under brutal Roman military occupation, the empire of God, will come. In fact, it is already here, despite how few people might attend church, how frightened they might be, how high the odds might seem against justice being achieved and peace restored.

The sower's chances of success are slim, and made more so in the story by the seemingly careless way in which he slings the seed about, on paths and rocks, around thorn bushes. This, it seems, is a very nonchalant farmer. But the story is saying not to worry about that. God's empire of justice and peace, of healing and wholeness, God's love story for all humanity will be told and will come to pass. Trust and relax in that promise. Start living as though it has already happened. Be sure that it has already begun.

But how, and where? Do we need to rush off to some holy place and do something special to experience that hundredfold promise of God? No, says this story. Stay where you are, doing what you're doing. This is not the Roman empire, which made its presence felt with great power, through marching legions, savage justice, dazzling architecture, awesome leaders. There are no emperor gods, no coliseums or crucifixions or military brilliance. We meet God's new order in the most ordinary, silent, simple things.

This parable is the first in a string of stories to show us how God comes among us: the sower and the seed, the leaven in the lump, the mustard seed in the garden, the employer paying his workers, the host at the dinner table, the trader on the road. It's in the way we garden, cook, clean, sew, entertain, do business, study, teach and organize; it's by doing all those ordinary things, faithfully and carefully and thoughtfully and generously and lovingly and creatively, that we meet God and God meets us.

And it is in those everyday encounters that the empire of God, in some mysterious way, slowly, silently and invisibly, takes over our lives and leaves us never quite the same.

It's like a garden you planted and never expected to grow, springing up all around you, swallowing you up in its luxuriance and beauty, returning you hundredfold. No matter what sort of gardener you are, no matter how many crop failures you've known, the miracle promised by this story can happen to you.

Storm is the norm

> The disciples are fishing at night on the lake of Galilee, far from shore, when the sea turns rough. They see Jesus walking towards them, on the water, and are terrified. Peter tries to walk to join him and starts to sink, until Jesus takes hold of him. (Matt. 14:22ff.)

When it comes to borrowing, telling, showing other people's stories, you do that at your peril. Whether it's men telling women's stories, Christians telling Muslim stories, tread carefully if you dare to tread at all. But there's no outcry, there are no complaints, when a pizza commercial borrows the church's story about Jesus walking on water. The ad shows a fisherman walking on water home across the lake to a hot pizza lunch. Where do you think they got that idea from?

The trouble with the wholesale theft of Christian imagery and symbols by the advertising industry is not that they borrow from the language of our Christian tradition. We don't have copyright control, and much of it was borrowed from Jewish and Near Eastern cultures anyway. The trouble is that there is no consultation or acknowledgment, not even much curiosity, about how that language might be used respectfully. These days, when films are made about indigenous cultures, there's usually some real effort to get the story right, as there was in *Dancing with Wolves*. But when anyone walks on water on TV, or parts the Red Sea, or ascends into the clouds, it's portrayed as something literal, even magical. Such biblical stories are filmed to elicit a response of amazement, shock, surprise. Christianity becomes something best handled by the special effects department.

At the start of the 21st century we have lost control over our heritage. "The Bible is the church's book" was the catch-cry of my theological college principal, Frank Synge. He would be turning in his grave if he could see the pizza ad I've described. Everyone but the church is putting a spin on our stories and symbols, from the cross used as costume jewellery to words like mission, ministry and charisma being taken over by the corporate boardroom. All this means that Christians have to decode their stories in order to get back to what they were meant to say.

So was this passage about water-walking a magic story for the church? Was it told to impress them that Jesus could do anything? I doubt that very much. You may choose to believe this story is literally true, but even if it is, it wasn't told to show Jesus as a superman, doing impossible things. That's not what Matthew intended, in a world where magic workers and miracle healers were a dime a dozen. More importantly, this is a story about discipleship and what it means to be the church and, in that way, it's a much harder story to accept. It would be far easier if all we were being asked to do was believe in miracles.

Jesus is talking to the still small and struggling community of believers. The boat is the enduring symbol of the church, and now of the ecumenical movement. It's not a cruise ship, but a little fishing trawler. And the sailor disciples are very unhappy. The wind is in the wrong quarter, they're a long way from the shore, their vessel is being battered about. Is this what it means to be the church, always caught up in a storm with the odds against you? It was tough and unsafe being Christian at the end of the first century, with political and religious hostility on all sides. And at the moment of this story, life was very hard. It was the fourth watch, the darkest hour, just before dawn. Yet it's precisely at the disciples' darkest hour that Jesus meets them, in an extraordinary and unexpected way that scares them silly.

This is a story about the way it is for faithful Christians, and has always been when we're doing our job. It's rough and uncomfortable, the odds are against us; the storm is the norm. Expect that. But you can also expect the God we know in Jesus Christ to meet us in the storm, whatever form that turbulence might take: illness, broken relationships, financial hardship, a future that looks bleak, a past that won't let us go. Whatever sort of storm we're sailing in, the story says, hold on, keep going and trusting that God will meet us.

That's what it means to be obedient. The word isn't so much about doing what you're told as facing the facts, paying attention to the ways things really are. Obedience is always a chemistry of realism and trust. We face up to the way things are, however bad, and hold out for the promise of a better way.

And just what is the storm that we are sailing in, right now, as the church? Where I live, it's certainly not persecution. The church is the safest of places, too often a haven to which we escape rather than facing the storm. One pervading storm we face in New Zealand is our irrelevance as an agency of change in society. We aren't connecting with the issues that make and break the lives of those around us, especially those under forty. And with that growing irrelevance goes an increasing media invisibility.

One of the beauties of belonging to the ecumenical movement is that our traditional logo is a small boat sailing in choppy seas. (It's time the waves were drawn in wilder, rougher lines.) But with that logo goes a huge responsibility. We must provide a place where all sorts of people, both inside and outside our churches, can find help to survive the storm they're sailing through. We must be a place that's known for addressing the world as it is, torn and broken by growing poverty, confused by false promises of a consumer heaven. We must use the freedom we have ecumenically to experiment with liturgy and music and educational programmes that let new people find meaning and order in the midst of great confusion. As a movement we sit on a treasure chest of rituals and symbols and beautiful forms, as well as shared wisdom and expertise.

Unlike some of our grander church buildings, the tent-like, temporary structures of the ecumenical movement don't serve well as sanctuaries and safe harbours from the storms of life. Our ecumenical role is to provide a place where people can learn from each other the skills of navigation in rough weather, where we test out new ways of staying afloat, where we try to walk as Jesus intends us to walk – confident and strong when the wind is against us, knowing we are not alone, relishing the challenge and the risk and the excitement of discipleship. Through our ecumenical networks we need to fill our churches with stories and symbols of faith that keep people sailing in the wildest seas and on the darkest nights.

Pearls not for sale or rent

> In a bracket of three parables, Jesus compares the kingdom of heaven to a merchant who finds a single pearl of great value and sells everything he owns to buy it. (Matt. 13:45-46)

The only disappointment at my thirtieth wedding anniversary celebrations was that nobody gave me or my wife any pearls. I looked up the list of anniversary presents and found that I couldn't expect any gold or silver or wood. But I was entitled to expect a pearl or two. It wouldn't have had to be one of those black Japanese pearls that I see displayed in local jewellers shops, secured behind thick plate glass and high-tech burglar alarms. The simplest cultured pearl would have been enough.

Because pearls are beautiful things, symbols of all that is gracious and lovely and of good report. A pearl, like few other single material things, has the capacity to sum up all that value in a single, lustrous, perfectly formed statement. Like a violin concerto, except you can hold a pearl in your hand. Like a wonderful flower, except a pearl lasts for ever and you can pass it on to your daughter and your granddaughter. A pearl of great price – the phrase conjures up for us much more than money. We're talking here about something exquisite. And as for a string of them, well, they defy words to describe their real value. No wonder Glen Miller and his orchestra called one of their all-time great numbers "String of Pearls". No wonder the opera that contains that famous duet is called *The Pearl Fishers*.

When Jesus told his own pearl story, recorded in Matthew's gospel, we tend to hear it as a story about fishing or searching for treasure, rather than about the treasure itself. The parable is usually interpreted as a challenge to spiritual treasure hunters to look harder, and when they find what they think is the treasure, to risk going broke and give up everything to secure the pearl of great price. The farmer sells everything he has to buy the field where the treasure is found. He doesn't want to be seen digging it up and taking it away without having gone through a real-estate sale. And the merchant, no doubt already a wealthy man, someone who had seen more precious stones than we've had hot dinners, sells everything he has to secure this pearl of great price. So work hard at growing in faith when you find it. Pray hard. Study hard. Serve others generously. Sacrifice your self-interest. That's the way this parable is usually interpreted. And fair enough.

Except that it sounds like advice some of us don't need. We're already getting more than enough of that encouragement from pastors and teachers, sports coaches, politicians and financial planners, not to mention a barrage of media advertising telling us to try harder and aim higher and eat better. What is the other question, not usually addressed, that this parable poses, namely, just what is this treasure that Jesus is talking about? What is the pearl of great price? It's as much a question for the wider community as it is for the church and the ecumenical movement.

For Jesus it was clearly the kingdom of heaven, which is better translated as the empire or realm of God, to draw the comparison that was overwhelmingly urgent to Jesus and his followers, suffering under Roman rule. Nothing irked a good Jew more than having his or her country occupied by a foreign army, and paying huge taxes to support an overseas emperor who defiled everything that was sacred and holy. The popular feeling against the Roman empire had grown so strong by the time this story was written down that there had been a Jewish revolution in Jerusalem. The Romans suppressed the revolt with great savagery, including the sacking of the temple in Jerusalem. So when Jesus talked about the empire of God as the pearl of great price, there was a real edge to what he offered.

His was a vision of the world that refused to divide people by gender or race or religion; a vision that created no outsiders. It was driven by generosity, forgiveness and room to start over again when we fail. It valued love above everything, and justice, which is love spread around evenly. In first-century Palestine, this vision was translated into a ministry of hospitality and healing and teaching that got Jesus crucified, such was the threat it posed. How is that same vision translated in our time, so that it has equal effect? To answer that question is to find the pearl of great price.

Today the ecumenical movement is threatened by those who want to practise new forms of exclusion, this time on grounds of sexual orientation, or doctrinal belief, or moral worthiness. There is a scary mood in some parts of our churches that wants to close ranks and paint the world out there as an evil place. I don't think we're going to find many pearls by following that approach. In the century ahead, we're going to have to be even braver in opening our ways of meeting and forms of worshipping so new people can find a vision of Jesus for themselves.

At Christchurch Cathedral, we're learning that we do best when we talk less and listen more, when we risk offering our treasures of liturgy, music and devotion to people who might not seem to appreciate or understand them, when we're willing to work in partnership with other groups we once saw as competitive or unfriendly, when we share ecumenically and cross-culturally in ways we once found too hard to attempt.

As never before, the church needs organizations to work from within at renewing, rethinking, redefining the old boundaries of faith, challenging all of us to see where the pearls of great price for our time might be hidden in our soil. For they will always be hidden, and found only by those who have courage and imagination and nerve. To lead that search is the true vocation of the ecumenical movement.

One o'clock, two o'clock, three o'clock rock

In Caesarea Philippi, Jesus asks his disciples who they think he is. Only Simon Peter gives a clear answer and Jesus names him as the rock on which he will build the church. (Matt. 16:13-20)

Do you remember the fashion a few years ago for pet rocks? You bought them in a nice box and carried them home where they never made a mess or a noise. Unlike other pets, you could give them away to friends. Someone made a lot of money out of pet rocks, but they didn't last. The joke wore thin. Perhaps we realized that rocks weren't as stupid as they looked. They deserved more than to be mocked in a box.

Rocks speak of everything that is solid and enduring and dependable, in and out of season, at one o'clock and two o'clock and right around the clock. "Rock of ages", we sing, when we need a little stability in our lives as we face crisis and death.

Drive through the high country not an hour from Christchurch, in New Zealand's South Island, and overlooking the highway stand the sentinel rocks of Castle Hill, and across the road the long line of the Southern Alps, where massive rock plates meet above the ground, exposing the foundations on which the country stands. These rock forms shape our common life in ways we're barely conscious of, as we drive past.

Rocks aren't always so dependable and reassuring – on the same high country road, the signs say beware of falling rocks, and a favourite gospel image is the rock that causes the proud to trip and stumble – yet they are usually associated with solid and enduring strength. A rock is what you need to build a community on, and to do that, Jesus chooses a fisherman called Peter. He gives him a name – Petros in Greek, Cephas in Aramaic – which literally means rock. The name Peter doesn't exist in the Hebrew tradition: Jesus invented it for him. He made him the Rock Man.

Now with the greatest respect, we have to ask whether that was a very clever thing for Jesus to do. Wouldn't James or Andrew or Mark, or even one of Jesus' brothers, have been a better choice? They all seemed to be reliable, balanced, dependable people. But Peter was headstrong and impulsive, anxious about his own importance, ambitious and unwise. He talked before he thought, and walked before he thought, even on water. Worst of all, he was unreliable. In a crisis, he let you down, not once but over and over again. He would even deny he knew you to save his own skin.

Peter the rock? You've got to be joking. Yet he was the one that Jesus singled out to address the question that had been worrying everyone for weeks? Like the disciples, we keep asking, "Who is this man?" and now Jesus asks the same question himself: "Who do you say that I am?" It's Peter who answers and is given the responsibility to build a community of people who share the answer: "You are the Christ, the son of the living God."

But can you believe anything Peter says? Would you buy a used car from this man? If you can see a problem here, then come further into the text and closer to this image of the rock, because it's going to get worse before it gets better.

The rock doesn't speak only of strength and dependability. More importantly, it speaks of the miracle of new life. Perhaps the most famous rock in the Jewish heritage was the one at Horeb that Moses was commanded by God to strike with his staff when the Israelites were dying of thirst. Moses did as he was told and a spring of living water gushed out that brought new life and hope. The people were asking, "Is God in our midst or not?" The water from the rock answered their question decisively, not least because the life-giving liquid sprang from such an outrageously unlikely place. When you look at rocks through the eyes of faith, you also get the miracle of new life, new energy, new hope.

And that's what Peter provided. So much so, that the church made a hero out of him, founded a city in his honour by taking over the capital of the Roman empire and giving him the title of His Holiness. Peter became a pope who wore fisherman's shoes and a gold crown.

Unreliable, up and down, on-again off-again Peter. What fights and factions must have swirled around him in the early church. Paul has some pointed things to say about him between the lines. "I have been told there are quarrels among you," he writes to the church in Corinth. "Each of you saying, I follow Paul, or I follow Apollos, or I follow Christ, or I follow Peter. Surely Christ hasn't been divided among you!" But in fact, he had.

Writing to the Galatians, Paul uses even stronger words. We recognize Peter as a "reputed pillar of our society" but in Antioch Paul "opposed him to his face because he was clearly in the wrong", changing his mind about circumcision, afraid of his critics, mixing with the wrong sort of people, vacillating, showing a clear lack of principle.

Peter the rock. Who would want to build a church on this man? Well, Jesus did. And it's the very same church we've got today, made of rocks that may look ordinary at best, downright unsteady at worst, but through which, nonetheless, the miracle of God's love and grace and new life can flow.

The first letter of Peter invites us all to take up this marvellous possibility of becoming rock men and rock women. "Come and let yourselves be built as living rocks into a spiritual temple," he writes. And if you find that prospect unlikely because you've been kicked around, overlooked and undervalued for too long, or if you feel too old or tired or busy to be much help to the church and the ecumenical movement, then remember, says Peter, that the living stone from which we draw our strength, Christ himself, was rejected and shamed and abused in unimaginable ways.

A cathedral such as the one in which I work is not a bad place to talk about living stones when you are surrounded by rock walls two metres thick and packed with rubble. There is a strong instinct in imposing places like cathedrals that suggests God prefers to deal with people whose motives are clear and clean. There is an unforgiving spirit that says if someone makes a mistake, we can never trust them again. There is a longing in holy places like this to idealize pure people and judge all those who fall short, to find some moral high ground on which to stand.

Not only is that a highly impractical way to run a cathedral – pure people are very hard to find – but it's also not very biblical or Christian, if we're to believe this story of Peter the Rock Man, an unlikely person being used by God in the most remarkable way. It's Peter who tells us that God brings new life despite our failures. It's Peter who tells us that the future does not belong to the smart, sensible, safe people who protect themselves and watch their backs, but to the ordinary folks who give of themselves generously, who get involved and, when they fall over, get involved again. It's Peter who tells us that we don't need to wait till we're pure enough or good enough to get involved in the loving, forgiving, serving, welcoming work of the body of Christ.

We don't have to wait to become living stones. God isn't fussy, says Peter the Rock Man. Miracles can happen, even through people like us.

What about the workers?

Jesus compares the kingdom of heaven to a landowner who hires two groups of labourers to work in his vineyard. The first group is hired early in the morning, the second near the end of the day. Both groups receive the same pay, much to the distress of those who worked the whole day. They complain bitterly to the landowner who warns that the last will be first and the first last. (Matt. 20:1ff.)

The parable of the labourers in the vineyard has been treated by the church like an old friend you take for granted. The usual interpretation goes something like this. This is a story about a landowner, even though it's called the parable of the labourers. And the landowner, of course, is God. The vineyard is Israel, or the church. The first lot of labourers are the Jews, the second lot are Gentiles, like you and me. The problem with us, in God's eyes, is that we grumble a lot. We're ungrateful for what we're about to receive, and when people alongside us receive more than they deserve then we huff and puff even more, full of our own self-righteousness.

But God doesn't work by our rules. God's grace isn't contained by our ideas of deserving or earning. God is not bound by fair trade agreements or union contracts. God's judgments aren't subject to the employment court. God's grace is distributed with a generosity beyond our understanding.

All that has been the stuff of sermons on this passage for most of the church's history and it's all perfectly sound theology. But is it what this parable is really saying? Is there something more going on here? It's a very special story, not repeated anywhere else, which is highly unusual, yet it's rated by even the most sceptical scholars as the most reliable of sayings, the most likely to have come from Jesus himself. So how consistent is it with the rest of Jesus's teaching? What precedes and follows this story?

Jesus is talking about rich people. He's just told the story of the rich young man who went away sorrowful, unable to become a disciple because he had too much to lose. And Jesus has just said that it's very hard for people who have a great deal and are determined to hang on it. It's like getting a camel through an eye of a needle. He's not against rich people. He's just saying that those who have most to lose find it hardest to follow him; and from those of us who have most, most is expected.

Then, immediately after this parable, Jesus goes on to talk about the journey to Jerusalem where he expects to die. The stakes in this story are very high.

Jesus is talking in this parable about a Jewish world, where the law was everything. And the law said very clearly that no one, however rich, had the right to talk as though he owned the land and could do what he liked. God owned the land, and every jubilee year those who had money should give those in debt a break and a chance to start afresh. No God-fearing landowner would have dared to talk as arrogantly as the one in the story.

Jesus is talking about real people in the real world. He himself came from the peasant class so he knew what it was like to live on the brink of poverty, in a country run by an occupying army and their client governors who milked the population for every coin and every crop they could secure. And he knew only too well what the life of a day labourer was like. It's been highly romanticized by Sunday school pictures of happy workers in the fields, but we know much more now about the sociology of first-century Palestine. Day labourers were men who had fallen off the cliff of society. When they couldn't find casual work, they had to beg on the streets, or join an outlaw gang. Even slaves were treated better because at least they were an investment. Day labourers were either peasant farmers who had lost their land through foreclosure on debt or they were the children who missed out on family inheritance. Either way they were desperate and expendable, constantly hungry, malnourished, diseased. Once they entered this class, their life expectancy dropped very drastically. The denarius they were paid for a day's labour was meant to sustain them for a day, but the work was spasmodic, limited to planting and harvest time. For most of the year they starved.

We know from the rest of his teaching that Jesus has highly biased and sympathetic views towards the poorest of the poor. They shall inherit the kingdom of heaven. The last shall be first. Blessed are those who have least. If this parable is at all consistent with the rest of the gospels then it has to be at least as much about the workers as it is about the landowner.

So what's it saying about them? They argue a lot, they are divided between themselves, which is exactly how the landowner likes them to be, because that way he can pick and choose them as it suits and arrange their payment as his mood takes him. And that kind of division is disastrous. The only hope for day labourers was to work together as best they could, under the protection of the Jewish law which did respect them, even if that law was often broken as it is being broken in this story. When the poorest in our society are divided and set against each other then their tragedy is multiplied a hundred times. We only have to look to East Timor to see that: a poor people trampled by twenty-five years of military occupation that encouraged and armed militia groups of local people to exploit their own, setting Timorese against Timorese.

The Jewish peasant audience that first heard this story would hear it very differently from us. They would recognize the desperate plight of all those day labourers, those who came early as well as those who came late. They would savour the irony and the warning behind Jesus's words, "The last will be first and the first last." They would be highly sceptical of the landowner's largesse, and they would certainly know that his line, "Friend, I am doing you no wrong", was anything but straightforward, tongue in cheek at least. The Greek word used for friend is about as unfriendly as you could find.

This is a parable that calls for a change of heart from rich and poor alike. It judges both groups and holds them to account, for both groups are capable of envy and selfishness, complacency and arrogance. But the parable has more to say. The poorest of the poor would have been encouraged by this story and its call to act together, for they knew it came from a man whose mother sang of a God who puts down the mighty from their seat and exalts the humble and meek; a man who opened his ministry with Isaiah's promise to bring good news to the poor.

To the privileged Jews of the day who relied on the Roman invaders to protect their exploitation of their own people, this would have been a subversive parable indeed. Not only for its criticism of economic systems that lock an underclass into poverty to balance the comfort of the rest, but also for its outrageous claim that everything we enjoy is a gift from God. We don't have the right to own anything – land, money, jobs – in any final sense. We are simply custodians, stewards of God's bounty, accountable to each other for each other's wellbeing, and expected to ensure there is enough for all.

That wasn't a popular message then. The day labourers had trouble hearing it. The landowners heard it and hated it. And it helped to hurry Jesus towards his death on the cross. It's not a popular message now, as the gap between the haves and the have-nots grows ever greater. The best place to start in addressing this crisis of a country out of kilter and a world out of balance is with Paul's question, "What do you have that you haven't received?" Only when we start to see our life as a gift, freely given, undeserved, unearned, can we start to find a way of moving ahead. And only when we start to see the world with such grateful eyes can we dare to take seriously what these words of Jesus might mean: "The last will be first and the first last."

When a friend of mine suffered a massive stroke some ten years ago now, his first question, over and over, was "Why me?" Then, after a time, he began to ask, "Well, why not me?" and started to argue the question both ways with God, finding as he went that it was his question and not God's.

Just imagine if we really believed God's love and grace didn't depend on what we deserved or how we behaved. Just imagine if the order in which we ranked ourselves and each other in didn't matter a scrap to God. Just imagine.

Does God need us?

While teaching in his home-town synagogue in Nazareth, Jesus is dismissed as a local boy and is unable to work miracles there. He responds by saying that prophets are despised on their home ground. (Mark 6:1ff.)

If you were hoping to represent your country at the next Olympic Games, and you haven't been told to start training yet, then it's probably too late. Once again, you've been overlooked. You've failed to get the recognition that you undoubtedly deserve. Someone who is better at promoting themselves will take your place. It's all very unfair.

The customary way of dealing with such failure is to hire a public relations firm to promote your case for you. Politicians do it. Job seekers do it. Corporations tendering for contracts do it. Schools do it. Even churches do it. It's still regarded as a little questionable to push your own barrow but paying someone to push it for you is increasingly acceptable.

But no good Jew in a first-century village would ever dream of any sort of self-promotion. The culture then, like many traditional cultures today, would never draw credit or importance to itself. That would be dishonourable. You wait for others to do that. Any advancement, any worthiness, any congratulation had to come from outside. So Jesus isn't being cute or bitter or even very profound when he says that prophets aren't recognized in their own environment. He's simply telling it the way it is. And the way it is for him.

Because it's clear between the lines of the story in Mark's gospel that Jesus didn't do very well in Nazareth, his old home town. Add all the versions of this part of his life together and you get a very human but not very flattering picture of a not very favourite son. We find out more about his family here than we do in the rest of the New Testament. We're told here, and nowhere else, that he has four brothers – James, Joses, Judas (not the one who betrayed him) and Simon – and that he had some sisters as well, though we aren't given their names. (Those church fathers who promoted the doctrine of the perpetual virginity of Mary a little later had difficulty with this passage, which disappears from later gospel manuscripts.) So here we have a boy from a big and perfectly ordinary family with no claim to fame or intellectual prowess. Hence the surprise in the questions that come: Isn't this the carpenter's boy, Mary's son? Where did this fellow get all this reputation he's building? Isn't he just one of us?

Remember that this gospel was written for the early church community some thirty years after the crucifixion when Christians were still trying to make sense of the Jesus story. They were struggling with the question of why God would allow him to die as a criminal in that most humiliating of public executions. They were sorting out stories of resurrection that didn't fit together neatly. Perhaps hardest of all, they were struggling with the rejection of Jesus by the very people who ought to have appreciated him best: his own people, his kith and kin.

Jesus might not have worried about this failure to be recognized for who he was, but the church did worry desperately about it, and still does. It makes a difference whether the community around you respects what you stand for. If people believe in you, if your public image is positive and confident, things happen. They didn't for Jesus, it seems. He healed a few people in his home town, we're told, but the text is amazingly frank. "He could do no deed of power" in that place.

This is a low ebb in the gospel story. Jesus is surrounded by disappointment, disbelief, failure and low morale. Yet he chooses this time to launch the first Christian mission, sending out his disciples to do what he could not do alone, empowering them to heal where he could not and to speak about God where he could not be heard. It's an astounding piece of timing. The mission does not depend on Jesus being successful, accepted and widely known – quite the reverse.

What the mission pivots on is the unqualified confidence that Jesus places in each of his followers, his utter confidence in them to be channels of God's love and grace. They are ordinary people with no great ability or special training. He's plucked them from the fishing boats and the tax offices up the road in Galilee. Now he commissions them to go out and tell the story and do the work he's begun, supremely confident that God will shine through their lives just as clearly, perhaps even more clearly, than God has shone through his own life. And that depends not on how well recognized Jesus is down home, but on how willing his followers are to be open and available to God. If they are, then God will guide and provide and produce results. They won't even need to worry about taking an outdoor coat for the journey or an extra dollar in their purse.

What we're offered in this passage is a radically new way of living, in which our own confidence and self-worth, our ability to make strong decisions and take bold initiatives, do not depend on other people's approval and recognition. These qualities come instead from the sure knowledge that each one of us is eternally valued and unconditionally loved by God, and that our offering of something worthwhile to the world can begin at any time, even in the not-so-successful times.

When I think about what keeps me going in the church and believing that the ecumenical movement still moves, I find, somewhat to my surprise, that it's neither the high days and holidays, nor the achievements we've enjoyed together. For me, the enduring things have been the glimpses of grace and generosity that I've been privileged to see in the lives of the ordinary people who make up the ecumenical movement, especially when they're dealing with grief and loss and illness and despair, when they are facing up to challenges in work and family life that make me tremble, when they push out the boundaries of what's possible and show me that I've set my horizons too close.

For that to keep happening, for those glimpses of grace and generosity to keep coming, we don't need anyone's recognition. It's more than enough to start with what we've got and who we are, and simply accept the confidence that Jesus offered to those first nervous disciples.

It's a dog's life

Jesus encounters a Gentile woman from Syrophenicia whose daughter is possessed by a demon. He is very rude to the woman when she seeks his help, treating her like a dog. Undaunted, the woman stands up to Jesus, convinced he can heal her daughter. Jesus is impressed, and the child is healed. (Mark 7:24ff.)

The images we choose to describe our heritage and our present reality can make or break us. The search for a common language to describe who we are and what we share as a community will determine whether we walk together or tear each other apart. We're a long way from finding that common language, yet our ability to find the right words to speak and be heard and be forgiven by each other is fundamental for finding faith in God and in each other.

That's a huge challenge for each of us and especially for churches, like New Zealand's, that claim to be bicultural. It was just as big a challenge for first-century Israel. What can we learn from the way they talked to each other then?

In Mark's gospel, chapter 7, Jesus goes to Tyre, a remote foreign region despised by every good Jew, and he meets a woman from Syrophenicia. Actually, she meets him, chases him down because her daughter is desperately sick. Jesus is unbelievably rude to her. His language his appalling. He calls her child the worst name he can find: "a dog", literally a puppy. To the Jews, dogs, like pigs, were ritually unclean; they were forbidden by the law even to touch them. Dogs were especially repulsive because they were known to eat human flesh: they hung around battlefields and places where people died away from home.

There might, however, be something else going on here, something ironic rather than simply literal. It's hard to imagine Jesus calling a sick child a little dog, and it's even harder to believe that the woman would literally accept such a label for she is a clever, proud and feisty woman, who will not allow herself be put down by a sharp-tongued Jewish rabbi, famous healer though he is. It's hard to translate something that was first said in Aramaic, then written in Greek and reaches us 2000 years later in a language twice removed from the original.

We do know that something subtle rather than crude is going on in this story. Listen to the marvellous interplay between these two staunch people: Jesus acting like a good Jew standing on his religious and cultural dignity; she acting like a good mother and refusing to be put in her place. He has nothing to lose but his pride; she has everything to lose, her daughter no less.

Tragically, this story is sometimes read as a crude conversation by smart people. I know people who have left the church because of the way this story has been misused and abused, as a weapon to make us all into miserable sinners, as a control mechanism to keep us suitably reverent and unquestioning in the way we talk about Jesus and who he really was.

But that's not what the gospel is showing us at all. What we read is the picture of a very human, very Jewish, some would say very proud male, being less than lovely and confronting a very determined, very brave, some would say very female, person. They meet awkwardly, reluctantly; they argue strongly, cleverly, passionately. And then something amazing happens. Instead of walking away as he was trying to do, ignoring her, dismissing her backchat as cheek, Jesus reverses his position. His harshest insult becomes his highest compliment. His exclusion becomes acceptance. And, far from rejecting her, he honours the mother and heals her daughter.

Instead of locking us into confrontation and mutual insults, the language in this story serves to liberate and redeem. It allows Jesus to get off the pedestal of his pride as a Jewish man. It allows the woman to break the mould of her foreignness and her inferiority. Through her words, Jesus glimpses the woman's courage, spirit and love. He honours that, and healing comes.

What are we to make of this story? It is telling us something about the way we can talk to God and to each other, especially those we don't like much or disagree with. It is suggesting we should try and use words honestly, truthfully, and always in a style that respects the other person's dignity and intelligence and allows a right of reply.

And in this conversation, Jesus is showing us, as he always does, the way we can speak to God. He's giving us permission to tell God just how we feel, however desperate or angry that might be. According to this story, God is never going to say, "Don't talk to me like that." We're being asked here to talk honestly, but also with great care. Irony, subtlety, gentleness, humour are okay in the divine conversation. Because the conversation with God (some people would call it prayer) is always happening in the context of a covenant, a committed relationship, so you can get away with admitting mistakes, and not taking yourself too seriously, and not watching your back because you're talking to someone who loves you enormously. A conversation with God is the one time you don't have to defend or explain yourself or impress anyone, let alone God.

Gospel-style conversations allow us to reposition ourselves, remove ourselves from the roles and positions into which other people lock us. Gospel-style conversations free us from speaking only in the way we're expected to, by virtue of our jobs, our gender, age, race or creed.

The gospel always gives us the right of reply, the chance to answer back, to say, "Hey, wait a minute, I'm more than that, I'm better than that, I don't have to live with that past, I can claim a future, and I don't even have to take myself too seriously. Call me a dog? Okay, well, supposing you let me lick up the crumbs under your table anyway. You can deny me a meal but you can't deny my dignity."

The Gentile woman who had everything against her and whose life was falling apart could claim that freedom. So can we. Because that freedom really is God-given.

What sort of a God is it that would take such cheek and run such risks? That is the most astounding part of this story. The gospel claim is that God behaves as Jesus behaves. Could it be that the God we worship is a God who meets us in the rough and tumble of the words we use to cope with each other? Could it be that God relishes being part of these conversations when we struggle to be human and honest and fully alive?

Could God be like that?

The blind see best

Bartimaeus, a blind beggar, hears Jesus approaching and demands mercy and healing. Jesus, impressed by his faith, heals him immediately. (Mark 10:46-52)

It may not be true for your country, but in Aotearoa New Zealand it pays to stay healthy and sane. It's also wise to have a good job, a manageable mortgage and an ambitious retirement savings scheme. I'm not sure how we manage to do that in a city like mine where 60 percent of the adult population live on $US10,000 a year. But never mind. The television ads tell us what we ought to be doing and show us all the wonderful things that could happen to our leotard-wrapped bodies if we ate enough wholegrain, low-fat, high-energy breakfast food.

In the meantime, even if you aren't becoming a healthier, wealthier, happier and more photogenic person, then don't get sick because society is growing increasingly intolerant of illness and disability and aging. The country simply can't afford it, we're told. There has to be a limit to all this suffering and dying. We can't stop it, of course, but we can try to ignore it. Recently, a little boy with cerebral palsy had to be taken to his first day of school in a baby carriage because the local authority couldn't provide a wheelchair. A young friend of mine suffered a stroke and couldn't get any physiotherapy for weeks because the hospital was short-staffed and the specialists were all on holiday.

Life in Aotearoa New Zealand these days is tough for those who aren't well or wealthy. It was even tougher for blind beggars in first-century Palestine. They, too, were ignored by the system of their day and left on the roadside to beg a living or die. That might seem unimaginable, but to those people it was business as usual. This man was blind because he deserved to be, and any illness, any physical blemish was a sign of unworthiness and a mark of God's judgment.

We don't believe that any more, thank God. We know we're all made equally in the image of God, all capable of realizing the same humanity, all deserving of the same dignity. It's just that political systems don't always seem to respect that. But the blind beggars won't wait. They have the nerve to keep making a noise and shouting out, "Have mercy on me." The disciples ordered this beggar to be quiet, and fair enough. The man has no manners, no sense of place, he doesn't seem to know who he's talking to.

Yet, oddly enough, he does know. This is the first time in the gospels that Jesus is recognized in public for who he really is without telling the speaker to be quiet, or walking away. The next time it happens, in the very next story, is the Palm Sunday procession, where not one man but a whole crowd recognize him with the same words, "Son of David", and Jesus doesn't argue.

It takes a blind beggar to start all this. Not the disciples who can't see for looking. Not the religious leaders who can't believe for all their knowing. Not the politicians who can't agree for all their negotiating. No, the pivot point in the gospel story, the bridge that links the healing and teaching ministry of Jesus with his entry into Jerusalem and all that follows is a blind beggar, a fellow called Bartimaeus, son of Timaeus. The drama of our salvation story is triggered by someone who can't see.

Because Bartimaeus is such a crucial figure, we know more about him than almost any other person in the gospels, certainly more than we do about most of the disciples. The only other figure who matches him in detail is the Samaritan woman at the well. The early church loved this story of the blind beggar and realized its importance. Bartimaeus became a representative figure and a model of trusting discipleship, someone who had nothing to lose, trusted Jesus completely, was forthright in his prayer and unconditional in his response. Healed by Jesus, and the word here means more than simply physical healing, Bartimaeus follows Jesus on the way, which means a lot more than a road. The early Christians were known as the people on the way, all the way to their own cross and resurrection.

Bartimaeus knows his limits, his devastating physical and social disabilities. He has every excuse to roll into a corner and give up. Instead he calls out to Jesus with great persistence. He seeks God's help, with everything he's got, and when it comes, he responds with everything he's got.

And Jesus recognizes something in this man that he hasn't found in even his most trusted friends and smartest colleagues. It's the same quality that he has already pinpointed in the Sermon on the Mount when he honours those who mourn, who have lost everything, who put others first, who seek peace, who give rather than take – to these people he promises the kingdom of heaven. What's more, he doesn't care who they are or what they look like, or how worthy they might be or how well behaved. None of that matters. In fact, those with the least going for them, those who have been battered and broken, seem in some mysterious way to be the most receptive to and perceptive about God's message. And just in case we miss the point, a blind beggar sitting in the gutter becomes the one who recognizes Jesus and walks with him on his final journey.

Now I don't know what those of us who are not blind beggars do about this uncomfortable story. One response is to go and sit in the gutters with the Bartimaeus figures of our time, and there are people like Mother Teresa and others who do that.

But there are other, equally valid, responses to this story, and they all involve laying ourselves open to the way God can break through all our normal and reasonable routines that keep us comfortable and safe and under control. God's truth has a habit of being packaged in dislocating and disconcerting ways: someone we thought was blind sees things we can't, someone we thought was dumb says things we need to hear, something we treated as ugly proves to be beautiful. Jesus took the risk of letting that happen to him. Let's take the same risk ourselves.

And a special welcome to the taxation department

> While walking on the lake shore, Jesus sees Levi, son of Alphaeus, a tax collector, and calls him to be a disciple. (Mark 32:13ff.)

It's a pity that Jesus had to choose his first disciples without the benefit of modern psychology and personnel management. If only he could have employed a good human resources consultant, he could have saved himself a ton of trouble.

The church's feast of St Matthias celebrates the last of the twelve apostles to be recruited. We know nothing about him, except that he was chosen by lot, the throw of a dice. The silence about Matthias might mean he wasn't up to much. After all, he was the replacement for Judas, who was up to a lot: betrayal, undercover spying, financial fraud which led to despair and suicide. Jesus would never have won an employer of the year award.

The gospel story about the recruitment of Levi is not quite as desperate, though, like Matthias, he disappears from sight and doesn't even make Mark's list of the super twelve. We know nothing about what sort of a personality he was, how he coped with stress, whether he was a team player, what his skills and professional training were. They didn't have the computer profiles and questionnaires we enjoy today but they did have shrewd interviewers and data-gathering systems. Remember, this was a country under military occupation so the networks of spies and intelligence gatherers were vast, on both the Jewish and the Roman sides.

Jesus could have checked up on Levi, son of Alphaeus, but there's nothing in the story to suggest that he was the slightest bit interested in Levi's personality or pedigree or performance record. The danger, in reading this story of sudden recruitment through twenty-first-century eyes, is that we clutch onto the wrong clues. For example, some commentators suggest that because Jesus was born and bred in Galilee, not far from Capernaum where this story takes place, he would have known Levi and his family anyway. But that is grasping at straws and inviting a psychological and biographical curiosity that simply isn't in the gospels. The writers weren't interested in the questions of personal motivation that obsess us today. They were writing theology, not biography. Their curiosity was about what God was up to in the world, how and where God was active and present in their midst.

All the story says is that Jesus recruited someone called Levi, very early in his ministry, that Levi was one of the very first disciples – number five, no less – and that Levi was a tax collector.

What's wrong with that? Some of my best friends work for the tax department, and although they get a rough time in the media they're not bad people and they've got an important job to do. What's more, if they don't collect the taxes from people who won't pay up, then the bill for those who do pay will only increase. But a tax collector in the first century was a despised figure – and for good reason: he worked for the hated Roman military invaders. And, to make it worse, in Galilee he also worked for Jewish traitors. In Judea, to the south, the Romans collected the tax directly; in the north it was collected through a series of puppet kingdoms. Capernaum was controlled by Herod Antipas who was spending a fortune on building a new capital in Tiberius down the road, a massive new public works programme of aqueducts, roads, buildings and lavish festivals. To pay for all this, as well as raise the levy that Rome required, the tax take in Galilee was gigantic, the equivalent of nine tons of gold each year.

And the people who extracted the money from the peasant farmers and the townspeople, always adding their own percentage on top of course, were the tax collectors. They did the dirty work and they were feared and hated for it. They were betraying their own people by aiding the enemy, breaking their own religious laws by extracting interest, dishonouring their culture by upsetting the social balance and pushing farmers and workers into poverty. On top of all that, they were often seen as frauds and crooks, running a personal extortion racket for themselves.

Jesus Christ started his ministry, announcing the good news of God's new reign, by recruiting a tax collector. Well done, Jesus. Did you know what you were doing?

Maybe Jesus did know. Maybe he deliberately set about showing that God was very different from the official version being promoted by the culture and religion of the day. For God had become tied up and tied down in a system of ritual purity and cultural honour and social roles that divided the world into insiders and outsiders, the clean and the contaminated, the honourable and the shameful.

Jesus sets out to challenge all that, out of his conviction that God's love is extravagant, unconditional, unselective, brimful and running over; that God's desire for justice and wholeness and dignity for everyone is not shaped by any of the systems we use to say who is in or out, worthy or unworthy, top or bottom of the heap. And, to make that point, Jesus chooses the people who were most despised to become his closest friends and followers: tax collectors, fraudsters, prostitutes, sinners. He even sits down to dinner with them all, we're told, just in case anyone is missing the point.

All this is very hard to swallow for any of us who have pretensions about the sort of people who ought to be attending our churches, these buildings that speak of the beauty and the dignity, the elevated honour and importance of God. It's so easy to slip into the mindset that says some of us deserve to be respected in the church and the ecumenical movement, to enjoy a special place and set the standards. But it's just such a mindset, however well intentioned, that lets us miss the point of this gospel story, which is to represent the radical hospitality of God, the unbelievable generosity of God's love and the utter trustworthiness of this man Jesus and his story.

If we're able to be as welcoming as he was, as focused on others, as confident that God really will be present no matter what, as sure that God really does bring new life when we stop holding on tightly to our old life, if we are able to trust this Jesus, who knows what he might be calling us to do, and in what strange company?

Music for maternity

In a song of praise and defiance, now known and sung as the Magnificat, Mary borrows the words of the prophetess Hannah to describe a God who upholds the humble, honours the promise of justice, and tears down the arrogant and the powerful. Mary's song comes soon after learning she is pregnant. She visits Elizabeth, wife of Zechariah, who confirms that Mary is soon to be blessed above all women. (Luke 1:46ff.)

I remember as if it were yesterday going to a Saturday afternoon movie as a ten-year-old, and paying for the ticket with a handful of pennies, because that was all the money I could find. Big, round, brown, heavy pennies. I was deeply embarrassed by having to pay in such clumsy coinage and tried to hide the pile I handed over. It was very uncool because it suggested you were poor and could hardly afford to go to the movies. Other kids in the queue had silver coins, even paper money. I longed to be like them. The sour taste of the envy I felt for the richer kids is still in my mouth.

Who are the lucky ones? Who triggers our envy? The saints among you can ignore that question, but the rest of us can linger with it for a moment. Much television advertising sends a subliminal message that there really is a group of God's favoured few who bask in the glow of good looks, great bodies, radiant health, happy families, glossy houses and gardens, driving cars that shine so bright you hardly need to turn the headlights on.

But in many countries, the economic surveys, the figures on health, housing and jobs tell a different story. The fortunate and favoured are fewer in number than we're led to believe, and infinitely harder to join. We know that most of those media messages are lies, yet we go on believing because we need to hold on to the myth that God really has singled out some special people over the rest of us. How else can you explain the rough deal we're getting? How come God lets us get sick and unable to afford the life-style we deserve? How come God lets bad things happen to good people and good things happen to people who don't deserve them? Is this any way to run a world?

The Bible is ambiguous on these questions. Jesus tells us that the rain falls on the just and the unjust; that every human life is known and valued, infinitely, by God; that we are made in the very image of God; that every hair on our head is numbered.

Jesus also tells us, through a series of parables, that God distributes grace according to a method that makes no business sense. God puts the first last, and the last first, hires the wrong people, keeps the wrong company, takes huge risks, gives and forgives with ridiculous generosity. All of this makes it very hard to know who God's favoured people are, if there are any. When Jesus is asked to sort this one out, he refuses to do so directly and tells stories instead.

His mother is more straightforward. She speaks more directly; in fact she sings what she feels about who God favours. It's not so much a logical explanation as a personal affirmation, a moment of revelation when those questions about what God is really up to suddenly dissolve because they have been reframed by an experience that changes the way you see the world. This is a brand-new experience for Mary, but it doesn't stop her borrowing the words from centuries before and using Hannah's song at the birth of Samuel. We call this song the Magnificat.

So what is God up to? Mary sings her discovery to the world. Newly pregnant, and frightened and bewildered by that, probably still a teenager, unmarried, just engaged, from a poor family in a poor region under military occupation, this young woman, on the basis of a conversation with an angel and an old cousin, bursts into an amazing song about the way God works, and who God favours.

"He scatters the proud, he brings down the powerful and lifts up the lowly, he fills the hungry with good things and sends the rich away empty." We sing these words so often that their shock is easily blunted. The poetry hides the political dynamite they hold. Surely such claims don't need to be made in democratic countries? We don't need to sing Mary's song, do we? True, there is poverty growing around us by the day, but that isn't something God cares passionately about, is it?

And here lies the problem of how to hear this song. Unlike many Bible stories, which weren't written to be taken literally, this one certainly was. The Jewish people, invaded and oppressed by a Roman army, exploited by a regime of quisling puppet kings, believed fervently that this suffering would soon end and they would once again be in control of their lives. And that's what happened, starting around the time this gospel was written down.

And the song is literally true because Mary is literally pregnant. She is about to give birth to an astonishing son and she has, in this story, some foretaste of a miracle that will bring us closer to what God is really like, closer than anyone else who has ever lived. When Mary sings that the world is about to be turned upside down, she is saying more than she knows.

But there's more to this song than the literal truth, for that runs dry after a while, as we see in those who use the song to proclaim a communist manifesto or a student revolution or a creed for a commune or the ideal welfare state or a perfect church. This is also a hymn of hope we can all sing, an epic poem about creation for everyone of us who wants to know what God is up to. It's like a universal charter for the reordering of the world.

We sense that when we hear the song but because we're so literal, so practical, we've lost the ability to respect what's going on. People in earlier times did better. They honoured the poor, gave special status to strangers, saw hospitality to travellers as a sacred duty, treated fools as holy. Because all these misfits, these inconvenient people, were somehow signs of God's own inconvenient presence in our midst. Our forebears couldn't explain this mystery any better than we can, but they did a much better job of respecting that mystery and making room for it.

And just what is this mystery? Mary, the young woman who had nothing and now has everything, sings about the promise of transformation we can all enjoy, all of us who don't have much ourselves. The only people who aren't included in this promise are those who feel they have it all, those who aren't hurting and have disconnected themselves from those who are. But if you're caught up in the lives of others, if you let yourself become involved and give of yourself wherever you can help and encourage others, then this is your song and these are your promises.

And they are very simple: that the God we meet in Jesus is an impatient God of justice who will not allow oppression and poverty to linger indefinitely in the land; that God will not tolerate the arrogance and abuse of power in any form, especially when it claims to serve the sick and the jobless, the poor and the homeless. Those who make that claim to serve others yet serve themselves first will reap the whirlwind.

There are some reassuring things about this discomforting song. It's sung by someone who started with less than any of us, in a society where to be young, poor, female and Jewish made life more difficult than anything we can imagine. If she can be exultant and passionate in her faith in a just God, so can we.

And her song is sung not just for the present order but for all eternity. Mary claims a time frame that no government, no authority figure can ever match. The promises God makes here are for all generations, to our ancestors and their descendants for ever. The revolution Mary sings of is not about to go away. It's not defined by the success of the United Nations or the World Bank or the outcome of the next election. This song tells of a new order that goes against the grain of all that's wrong with the way things are.

A young woman's song shows us the way it's going to be, one day.

Morning glory

Jesus borrows a fishing boat from which to address the crowds, then tells Simon the fisherman, who had been casting his nets unsuccessfully all night, to try again. Simon does so, with some reluctance, and the catch of fish is huge. (Luke 5:1-11)

There are lots of hymns about the glory of the morning. But they're hard to sing if you've had a rough night and the day ahead is full of difficult jobs and even more difficult people. Bright morning hymns are hard to sing without a decent breakfast of grilled kidneys and bacon and eggs, with perhaps a little fried bread on the side. Even then, you may not be in the mood.

What does help is to walk across a park and see the sun suddenly break through the clouds. It splashes patches of luminescence across the grass and the trees. The morning comes alive with colour. Someone you pass most days without a word says good morning, and you think as you walk of something really delicious to cook for dinner.

When all these things come together in a conjunction of surprise and delight, the once ordinary morning is suddenly transformed. This happens not because you're clever or worthy or deserving or even well organized. The only thing you've done is let yourself be open to what happens.

Luke's gospel story is about such a morning. It begins with all sorts of problems. The code word for problem in this context is "crowd", this huge and growing, endlessly demanding, shamelessly hungry and intrusive, constantly pressing and completely fickle force. One minute the people love Jesus, he can do no wrong. The next minute they want to tear him apart, and finally it is the crowd that chants, "Crucify him, crucify him."

When Jesus isn't teaching, debating, feeding, healing, being followed by crowds, he's hiding from them, trying to keep his distance. Here he acts in an impromptu sort of way by borrowing a boat from some disgruntled fishermen, who are washing their gear after a miserable night. And from his temporary platform just offshore, under difficult conditions, Jesus makes do with what he's got and for a time teaches this noisy, pushy, querulous audience.

Then he turns to deal with the fishermen whose boat he borrowed. He's probably met them already for the day before he heals the mother-in-law of a fellow called Simon, but there's no record of any more formal invitation in Luke's gospel. Jesus meets these disciples at work, doing the washing up, in their boats and their smelly work clothes, just as God called Moses while he was tending sheep and Gideon while he was beating wheat and Isaiah while he was on duty in the temple.

And, as with other invitations that God makes to other disciples-to-be, the first reaction is often grumpy and off-hand.

> "Have another go," says Jesus to the fishermen.
> "What do you think we've been trying to do all night?" says Simon.
> "Well, try again," says Jesus.
> "If you say so," says Simon, as if to say, be it on your head, you're wasting our time.

All of that part of the story sounds very familiar: making do with the inconvenient, uncomfortable, overcrowded and pressured way things often are; dealing with people who don't know what they want one minute and want too much of us the next and are not very thoughtful about how they ask. This is life as it is. These are people as they are. You could round up a crowd that behaved just like the one in this story, and you could name a dozen new disciples who were just as irritating and demanding and reluctant and unsuccessful as those fishermen. We might even have to count ourselves among that number.

It's an unlikely way to begin a story about a miracle, but that's the way God's miracles work. They don't pop out of the clear blue sky. The people they happen to don't wear angel's wings and sweet smiles and medals for good behaviour. The miracles happen in the midst of the hassles and the pressures that frame our lives. They're not divine inventions out of nothing, they're not magic tricks. The God we know in Christ works by transforming what is already there, bringing the raw material of creation together in ways we'd never experienced before, letting us see it in ways we'd never imagined it before, enabling us to sense and know it in forms we'd never thought possible. It's brand-new, yet still recognizable. It's overwhelming, yet we're still able to cope and comprehend – though only just. It's like the morning sunlight that floods the world around us, like the first morning of the new day.

A month ago, the son of an old friend was dying, his medical prognosis quite impossible. And every night for weeks, his young friends encircled his bed in the intensive care unit and prayed and sang quietly. Yesterday I heard he's sitting up and working on his laptop, giving cheek and demanding decent food.

For those who ask and wait for justice and healing and restoration and new life, God's generosity is excessive and overwhelming. The nets in our story are stretched to breaking point, the boats are starting to sink with the weight. If we open ourselves to the possibility of getting more than we asked for and far more than we bargained on, if we take the risk of being overwhelmed by God, then the response that comes from us may well need to be equally generous – we give more than we can afford, we love more than is safe, we work harder than is sensible. That's the risk involved in letting God transform us. The fishermen left everything, we're told, and followed him.

This gospel story launches us into the realm of courageous Christianity and high-adventure ecumenism. If we think we're too old or too tired or too stupid, or don't believe enough to take the risk of entering that realm, then we're missing the point of this story. None of what happened depended on the disciples being eager or well prepared or in control or even very polite. Their only qualification was being open to transformation – the miraculous way God works in taking what is ordinary and opening our eyes to its extraordinariness.

It's not a matter of adding something that wasn't there. It's a matter of bringing out what was there all along, what we couldn't see for looking: the sudden glimpse of courage and grace and humour and strength that we meet in people we've known for years and taken for granted, the news story that opens a window of respect on a cause we've had no time for, the experience of a morning that becomes for us the first morning.

That's the stuff of transformation. That's the way God works.

A God of great expectations

> Jesus is surrounded by a huge crowd desperate to be touched and clamouring to be healed. In his first major teaching session in public, popularly known as the Beatitudes, he blesses those who are poor, hungry, sad or rejected, and curses those who think they have everything. (Luke 6:17ff.)

Like many other former colonies of Europe, New Zealand is a country built on great expectations. Our forebears from Europe didn't come here because they were happy and successful back home. They came because they expected a better deal: better food, better housing, land they could afford to buy, jobs that might give dignity and decent wages, and a future that would be good for their children. The marketers of the New Zealand Company, which organized the immigrants, raised those expectations shamelessly, promoting a land of promise, an El Dorado.

Those very early and quite impossible expectations were disappointed. They got many New Zealanders off on the wrong foot, not because we were so hopeful, but because we were hopeful about the wrong things – getting rich quickly whatever the cost to the landscape and the people who were here before us. We started to expect that we were entitled to security and comfort, that we didn't need to be our brother's or our sister's keeper. Our expectations had to be painfully readjusted by depression and war, racial conflict and economic restructuring that tore all our old security blankets to shreds. Our expectation tank can soon run low.

Until we come across a passage like the story of the Beatitudes in Luke's gospel. It's a story all about dealing with great expectations. They come from two groups: a large gathering of disciples and a huge crowd from all over the region. Some of them would have been walking for weeks to get there. They were poor people, sick people, psychologically tormented people, people desperate for all sorts of reasons – burdened by poverty, illness, grief, social rejection. Everyone in the crowd, we're told, was trying to touch Jesus. Can you imagine the frenzy of that scene? These were people who had nowhere else to go. The intensity of their expectations would have been strong enough to smell in the air.

Most of us are afraid of great expectations. If we hope too much we might be disappointed. If we invest too much trust in someone else, we might be let down. If we reach out too far, we might fall over. If we give too much of ourselves and what we have, we may never get it back.

Jesus is never afraid of great expectations. He meets them head on, respects their intensity, revels in the passion and the excitement they produce, and adds some more of his own. Put your trust in this man and you'll get it back a hundred-fold. But you'll hardly ever get it back in the form you expected.

We're not told much about just what Jesus did that day, how many he healed. He certainly wouldn't have cured them all but he did speak to them all, so everyone could hear. What he did give them, every one of them, was an unexpected answer to their very predictable expectations of being helped and healed and fed and paid and accepted.

What Jesus gave them was a blessing. Even though what people came for was something more basic, such as pain relief, Jesus simply offered them a blessing.

In truth, there's nothing more basic than a blessing. It may be the most practical thing that we can ever give each other. Because you can't give people blessings unless you have first accepted them and connected them with all that is good and true and beautiful.

A blessing is a way of saying that you're valued, that you count for something in the scheme of things, that you have a place to belong and stand tall. The God we know in Jesus Christ doesn't dial us directly, but speaks through us and the whole creation. We're the channels of God's blessing. That's the job we've been given as people made in the image of God. We can never do it half-heartedly. We're either a blessing or a curse to each other, and we can be a blessing only if we know we are blessed ourselves.

And that's what Jesus did to this desperate crowd: he blessed them. Blessed are you who are poor, you who are hungry, you who are weeping, you who are hated because of what you stand for. You're blessed. You'll know what heaven is like. You'll dance for joy very soon. And for those who have it all, who don't need God's blessing because they have already blessed themselves and no one else, the self-satisfied ones, Jesus gives only a curse – the curse of having no expectations about the future. Nothing to hope for. No glimpse of a better way.

If that's your problem, then this story is advising you to start dreaming immediately. Set some goals quickly for how you might live more generously, creatively, compassionately. If it's security that's preoccupying you, then go out and take some risks. If you're holding on too tightly, find something to give away. But if your problem is the opposite, if you know you're poor, or ill or very sad, if you hunger after a better way, a fairer deal, if you're already taking risks and giving generously to others, then this passage is good news, the best news, better than any cure or payout or prize you could imagine. The good news is that you're blessed by God, in the sense of being accepted, loved and honoured. You've been given, freely and unconditionally, the right to be happy until it overflows inside you.

I've met some really sad people recently, but some of them have told me that in the midst of their grief they have been surrounded by overwhelming support and love. And, in my work, I've meet some very desperate people, but some of them have given me glimpses of courage and humour and grace that I know I could never muster up myself, and the strength they give me defies any words I can find.

If you dare to come to God with great expectations, if you can summon up the patience and the nerve to risk God's reply coming to you in surprising ways, then you're very liable to being greatly blessed. Take the chance. You have absolutely nothing to lose.

Sense from nonsense

In order to humiliate him, the Sadducees confront Jesus with trick questions about marriage laws in heaven. He turns the debate into a lesson on law and grace. (Luke 20:27ff.)

The Owl and the Pussycat went to sea
In a beautiful pea-green boat.
They took some honey, and plenty of money,
Wrapped up in a five-pound note.
The Owl looked up to the stars above
And sang to a small guitar,
"O lovely Pussy! O Pussy, my love,
What a beautiful pussy you are."

What do that poem and the gospel story of the Sadducees trying to trap Jesus have in common? Not much, on the face of it. Not much more if you dig deeper. The owl meant what he sang to the pussycat. The Sadducees didn't mean what they said to Jesus. It's as contrived a piece of questioning as anything in the Bible.

But, to modern ears, both the story and the poem are nonsense on first hearing. The poem is silly but fun. The story is silly but serious. It's all about a group we know nothing about, worrying about something we never give a thought to, within a legal system that no longer applies, asking questions they don't really mean, posed to ensure there can't be an acceptable answer. The real agenda here is humiliation, defamation, religion used as a weapon to control and destroy. But even that isn't clear to the first-time reader of this story. To most of us, this passage simply doesn't connect with anything that makes any sense today.

Except that there may be people who have been married several times or enjoyed several long-term relationships and worry about what will happen when they die. Will there need to be a tribunal in heaven where the chief angel sorts out which relationships still rule, or perhaps works out a roster where you spread yourself between old loves throughout eternity? The mind boggles at the possibilities. What happens to those who haven't found the perfect partner in this life so are looking forward to better luck in the next? It's a nice question but it misses the point of what Jesus is saying here.

Happily for all of us, he's saying that eternity is not bound by our institutions and covenants, however worthy they might be. Heaven will not be framed by the way we are now. There's no simple continuity between this life and the next; it's not a matter of slipping through a door to the other side where life and relationships will be more or less the same as we know them, only with brighter lighting and without housework and gardening.

Eternal life will be altogether different. The promise is not of resuscitation but of resurrection, of being transformed by the presence of the living God whom we will see no longer as through a glass darkly, but face to face. So there is that reassurance in this story. It's no comfort to those who want to get heaven sorted out before they arrive, but for those who are looking forward to something very different from the way things are, it's a great relief.

Good news, but not the main news of this story. The nonsense remains of these Sadducees, out to humiliate Jesus, asking questions about heaven that they don't mean and they know can't be answered. The Sadducees didn't believe in heaven. They were the Jewish party that argued against any sort of resurrection, because it was not promised in the law of Moses. In fact the law of Moses made resurrection impossible because it advocated levirate marriage, adopted by Moses from a widespread practice in Near Eastern cultures whereby a dead man's brother was legally entitled to take over the widow in order to produce children and ensure that the inheritance of the male household was continued and preserved. That law is primary, said the Sadducees. Imagine the log-jam it would create in heaven, so there can't be one, they argued. The whole debate might seem like nonsense to us. It would have had a slight air of unreality even to people in the first century, less zealous than the Sadducees with their tricky arguments. The temptation then, and even more now, is to walk away from all this foolishness.

One reason that so many people walk away or walk past the church is that they see us as still locked into such silliness: debates that don't go anywhere, doctrines that don't connect with our experience of life and death today, promises of salvation that don't relate to those things that liberate and nourish us day by day, meal by meal, laugh by laugh. But the challenge to every community of faith is to linger over these stories in scripture, to pray that God will break them open to us and let them speak afresh for all their quaintness and their seeming silliness. For they do contain the seeds of life eternal and the signs of life in all its fullness.

So what is Jesus telling us in this non-sense story? What's really going on? Well, he's being confronted by people who don't like him very much, who would, in fact, like to get rid of him. It may be personal but, more importantly, it's a clash of systems and values: the old law of Moses reserved for some versus the new law of grace and love open to all.

The confrontation takes the form of questions designed to demean Jesus, to strip him of his dignity as a teacher and a person. In a society defined by honour and shame, the Sadducees are out to destroy him as surely as by any physical stabbing. So the stakes are very high. Jesus has every reason to walk away from this one; for his own safety he should.

Instead he meets these critics on their own ground, inside their own arguments, quoting scripture back at them. Have you forgotten Exodus chapter 3, he demands? These authorities you cite – Moses, Abraham, Isaac and Jacob – they're not dead. Their words don't weigh us down. They live in God because the God we're all talking about is the God not of the dead but of the living.

And what's more, you can do what you like to demean me, but you won't draw me into anything that demeans you. I'll meet you as you are, even if you're trying to destroy me. Demand that I walk a mile with you and I'll walk two. Ask for my shirt and you can have my coat as well. Slap my face and I'll invite you to do it again. And even though I'll meet you anywhere and walk with you, wherever you are, however ambiguous and negative that may be, I'll find a way, with God's help, to go beyond wherever you are, for your sake and for mine. Because God doesn't intend us to live in argument and tension and duplicity. All our relationships are meant to let us see the best in each other, to expect even more than we can imagine or desire, to trust that all will be well, to err always on the side of generosity, to forgive and move on, to celebrate what unites us as the stuff of life, to make sure that what divides us remains secondary and unimportant, because it is the stuff of death.

How can we be sure that such an approach will work? Because the God who sustains and nourishes all things is the God of the living, not the dead. In this God, says Jesus, we are all alive and will live on in some mysterious way, into eternity itself. And there are no limits on where we can encounter this living God, even in the midst of encounters that seek to demean and destroy, even inside arguments with Sadducees, and governments and church conferences and ecumenical meetings that cannot agree. Because there is no pure place to stand to meet this God who works for good in all things. There is no special brand of people this God uses to do the work of love. There is no nonsense great enough to stop God making some sense out of it, bringing some grace, some hope, reclaiming some dignity.

Never mind the culture, grab the text

> John the Baptist declares Jesus to be the Lamb of God and sees the Spirit descending on him like a dove when he is baptized in the River Jordan. These events attract disciples to Jesus, notably Andrew and his brother Simon Peter. (John 1:29ff.)

The newspaper reviewer took a bet both ways on the annual local Proms concert. It's modelled on the annual event in the Royal Albert Hall in London where the audience wave Union Jacks and sing along to "Land of Hope and Glory", blending traditional British empire patriotism with a good time, in a tongue-in-cheek sort of way. The reviewer offered not one but two assessments. This, he said, was a shamefully unfashionable, obsolete and out of place concert, with music to make everyone but Colonel Blimp cringe. Or, he added, this is a wonderfully romantic and enduring celebration of a musical and cultural heritage. Same event. Two radically different ways of experiencing it.

John's gospel story of John the Baptist baptizing Jesus and spreading the word about him is often sold to congregations as one of the great recognition stories in the Bible. Divine insight comes down quite literally like a bird from heaven. This is the territory of angels speaking, just like the Christmas Eve story of the shepherds on the hilltops outside Bethlehem, suddenly overwhelmed by the sound of heavenly choirs singing.

Here we have the greatest prophet of the day, somebody we know a lot more about as the result of archaeology and discoveries like the Dead Sea Scrolls and the new work on the Essene Community, a radically alternative Jewish renewal movement. This revolutionary figure, with a huge personal following, is giving up his claim to religious leadership and handing over his authority to an unknown young teacher from Galilee.

And why? Because God had spoken to John directly. He had seen with his own eyes, at the moment when he baptized Jesus, a heavenly sign of a dove, and heard a heavenly voice. What's more, John passes on this discovery to two of his own disciples who in turn pass the word on to their friends and brothers and they too experience this divine recognition. One of them sees so clearly that he becomes the rock on which the church is founded.

It's about as clear as you could imagine. If a politician got that sort of multi-party endorsement, he or she wouldn't have to bother about campaigning in the next election. It would be like a political opposition leader saying publicly that he or she would rather like the prime minister or the president to keep the job for another term. It was an amazing endorsement for Jesus to receive inside the religious politics of the time. Even the title itself, "Lamb of God", carried an authority that seems to have commanded instant respect. Everyone knew that the lamb was the symbol of sacrifice and everyone knew that Jesus was to make the greatest sacrifice of all. If there are any lingering doubts about who Jesus really is, then this story ought to clear them away.

There is, however, another way of reading this story that isn't nearly as clear. Here you have John, the cousin of Jesus, baptizing him and saying "I don't know him", even as he bestows on him a divine title. And a little later, after all this is over and John has been sent to prison for stirring up the crowds, he sends out his followers to check out again who this fellow Jesus really is. A story of recognition becomes a story of confusion.

As for the image of the Lamb of God, it's difficult to connect with, especially if you're a meat-eater or, in a different way, if you're a vegetarian. But it would also have created a problem or two for those who first heard it, because lamb was not at all a normal image of sacrifice. Bulls, goats and sheep were prescribed by Jewish law as suitable animals for sacrifice, but never lambs. The connection here is with the lamb that was eaten at the Passover festival, but that has nothing to do with taking away sin, let alone the sin of the world.

And when you read this story closely, all the testimony has a very second-hand feel about it. Unlike the other gospel accounts, the baptism of Jesus is not described directly, but only as John remembers it, and the divine voices and symbols he saw and heard were not, apparently, seen and heard by the others on the riverbank, not even the disciples closest to hand. By the time the story of who Jesus is gets to Peter, it's already third-hand.

Now I don't know what your experience of third-hand messages is like. Maybe you're surrounded by people with perfect diction, impeccable recall and photographic memory, but where I live and work, anything second-hand usually spells trouble and third-hand is danger territory.

How do we read this story? Is it about recognition or confusion? Living with holy certainty, or holy ambiguity? The church is deeply divided on this question, but so is the whole of our society. Because we're increasingly divided into two distinct cultures: one that values certainty, clarity, being positive and knowing what's going on, no matter what, and another that respects complexity and ambiguity, accepts not always knowing as no bad thing and welcomes doubt rather than ignoring it. Whichever culture we belong to, we bring those values with us to this text and start looking for the common ground the story provides.

Whatever else it is, this gospel passage is at least a story about Jesus, a first-century Jewish rabbi, being recognized by all sorts of unlikely people, including his competitors, some of them very religious, as someone who pointed them to God in a completely new way. And all this happened through the same sort of process by which we learn important things about each other and the world – namely through letting ourselves be surprised by truth that comes in ways we don't expect; and through stories and opinions and endorsements that we get from others and have to trust; and in ordinary, everyday times and places.

My favourite line in this story is when the two disciples go to see Jesus. "It was four o'clock in the afternoon," we're told. Four o'clock – no great symbolic meaning here. We may as well be told the colour of the wallpaper. It serves simply to anchor the encounter in the ordinary stuff of the humanity and the history we share with Jesus then and Jesus now. This is a story in the continuous present. As then, so now. Jesus with us. God with us. No tricks, no magic mirrors.

The holy in the human, in the daytime of our confident, sun-lit lives and in the night-time and the darkness of our fears.

Both ways of reading this story, as divine recognition or divine uncertainty, have to cope with the fact that it is grounded in our common humanity and our common history. And we don't have to weed out all the confusion and the second- and third-hand complexities before we accept the story as reliable.

After all, the story ends with Jesus choosing someone who proved to be the most impetuous and unreliable of the disciples, someone who betrayed him three times and deserted him at his death, to be the rock on which the church was built. Silly old Peter, the pumpkin eater – he could have been, and was for a while, a figure of ridicule. Yet he became Peter the rock.

Is that any way to build a church and an ecumenical movement, relying on ordinary people trusting each other, even when they let each other down, coming and going, questioning and chatting, getting entangled with relatives and friends? Is that any way to build a church? Is that any way to find out what God is up to?

You bet it is.

The God who loves weddings

> The wine runs out at a wedding that Jesus attends with his disciples and his mother in Cana in Galilee. His mother organizes Jesus to help. He orders six huge jars to be filled with water and turns it into superior wine. (John 2:1ff.)

Tony and Mary are to be married soon. Their wedding plans started out very modestly. They hadn't planned to get married at all. Money was short, it would be a hassle and they were happy enough, living together. Then things started to snowball, all sorts of people wanted to be involved. Now they're expecting a hundred and sixty guests or more. There is to be a bridal party of nine and the page-boy wants to wear yellow. This wedding is going to be something special.

There's nothing special about the way John's gospel begins. No Christmas story: no baby in a manger, no wise men or shepherd or heavenly choirs. In this version they seem to be on holiday. All you get in this book is an introduction to John the Baptist, then we attend the baptism of Jesus and recruit the first disciples. There's nothing at all about the man's background. He's simply dropped into the narrative like a passer-by: "The next day John saw Jesus coming towards him." Who's this?

And so the greatest story ever told gets underway. Not with all the apparatus of Epiphany, but through a series of signs that show us who Jesus is by having him take part in ordinary events of life in Palestine: having dinner, catching fish, getting sick, having a drink on a hot day, arguing with the bureaucrats and first of all, as sign number one, going to a wedding. There's no better place to begin, John is saying, than with a wedding.

Because then, as now, weddings always end up as great occasions, even if they do start small. Tony and Mary's wedding will last half a day and a night. First-century Palestinian weddings usually went for a week. It was hard to keep anyone in the village away and everyone in the extended family simply had to attend. Because in every Jewish marriage, the future of the families on both sides was at stake. All matches were arranged by relatives, the couple would be as young as eleven or twelve and the bride had to be paid for: a large

dowry would have already been handed over. It was a financial deal equivalent to a house mortgage and the honour of
the families demanded that everything was done on the most
lavish scale affordable. A wedding that didn't go right would
result in political fall-out and lasting social disgrace. Culturally speaking, a wedding had the importance of an international football match.

And it's at a wedding that Jesus chooses to show himself.
He goes along with his mother and his friends, not to perform
miracles but to have a good time; in fact it seems he just
dropped in along with about seven others. We know Jesus
liked these occasions. He compared himself to children playing at weddings, unlike John the Baptist whom he compared
to children playing at funerals. Marriage is a favourite
metaphor and Jesus often uses the word bridegroom to
describe himself; his ministry is likened to an extremely long
wedding feast. So long as I'm around, he told his friends,
enjoy yourselves. Forget that stuff about fasting and looking
gloomy.

This wasn't a special wedding. No one special lived in
Cana of Galilee anyway and the fashionable set got married
in Jerusalem. This was simply meant to be a great occasion
for everyone involved and for as long as the wine held out.

But here's where a straightforward story starts to slide off
the rails. They do run out of wine early on but, instead of asking the guests to bring their own, the mother of Jesus gets
involved. Archbishop William Temple believes that the
unexpected arrival of Jesus and his friends puts a strain on
the supplies and Mary feels responsible for that, as mothers
do about the unplanned actions of their children. Anyway,
their conversation is unintelligible to anyone else, as it often
is between mothers and sons. It's Mary who starts issuing the
orders.

And something quite outrageous happens. It's not that
Jesus simply tops up the supplies. If you take the story literally, he produces some 700 litres of new wine, and top quality wine at that, but maybe we're not meant to take that figure seriously.

What the story does want us to take seriously, and the reason it's told at the very start of John's gospel, is the way God works in the world – through Jesus in this case, later through his first friends, the disciples, and now through us, his later friends.

The formula is simple enough. If you're a friend of Jesus don't spend too much time in holy places, but get out into the world of weddings, parties and celebrations, and expect to see God at work in the midst of everything that's going on, even if it's something as silly as the wine running out. Act as though that can happen. Help to make it happen as best you can and, even more important, stay open and available to God, because you never know what's going to turn up.

The thing we learn from the Jesus story is that God has to work with what's at hand. The story doesn't say that they sent out for something special. Jesus used the water on hand, the water that would otherwise have been kept for washing up. And Jesus didn't make a big fuss about solving the problem. The important people at the wedding, the guests, even the chief caterer didn't realize what was going on. Only the waiters knew that something extraordinary had taken place.

Most of the time God works silently, unseen, without credit, because God is working through people like us. And when something extraordinary does happen, when new life, new hope, new energy are found, when healing takes place and grief is worked through and pain is eased, when forgiveness is given and received and grace is experienced as surprise and delight, then we're inclined to forget this comes from God. We've even been known to take the credit ourselves.

But we receive nothing that we haven't been given by God, and we need to be clear about that, in the little things. Because one of these days, we're going to be overwhelmed by a gift of grace on the scale of 700 litres, full measure, pressed down, running over. We're going to find ourselves overwhelmed by love and grace that know no limits.

Believing is a hard day's work

The crowd find Jesus in Capernaum and ask for a sign to prove his divine authority, just as their forebears had received bread from heaven. Jesus replies that he is that bread of life. (John 6:24-35)

On the face of it, it's a very strange way to be talking about faith in God. We're used to thinking of faith as something that happens to you, whether slowly or suddenly; or as something you remember and reach for from earlier in your life. But faith as something you work for? What does that mean? Faith as work! Isn't that asking for trouble in a world where too many people have no rewarding work and a few have too much? Work in our time is defined as something you must struggle ever harder to qualify for and, when you get it, takes you somewhere better. Read the situation-vacant ads in the newspapers that promise promotion, health insurance, overseas holidays. Are those the things that Christian faith delivers when you work for it?

If it's any comfort, first-century Palestinians had just as much trouble sorting out what Jesus meant when he said that faith is work. Paul said it's faith, not work, that will save you. James said faith without work is dead. But Jesus said faith is work.

Let's check the context of these words. The crowd has just experienced the feeding of the five thousand where they didn't have to do anything and found there is such a thing as a free lunch. This is religion of the signs-and-wonders variety and they are hungry for more.

They want a god man who can leap tall buildings in a single bound and snatch children from under the wheels of runaway buses. *Jesus Christ Superstar* shows us the god that we know you are and the whole world will believe when they see you on the evening news.

But Jesus refuses to oblige. What the crowd doesn't know is that the age of signs and wonders is coming to an end. It was over by the time this gospel was written down at the end of the first century. It's the Holy Spirit that leads people into faith. Jesus makes the point most dramatically in the story of doubting Thomas in the upper room after the resurrection. "I won't believe unless I can touch you," says sign-hungry Thomas. "Okay," says Jesus. "Go on. Stick your finger in my wounds. Stick your whole hand in, if you can." There is a savagery in the language of that story. Jesus is taunting his disciple for the crudity of the faith he's trying to prove. Thomas should know better. The age of signs is over.

It's over, too, for the crowd in this gospel story. Faith is not something you can have instantly, for short-term satisfaction, like a take-away meal. It's a food that nourishes for ever; it gives life to the whole world.

So how do you find this faith if it doesn't switch on like a heavenly neon sign? What sort of work is required to produce this faith? It's all very well for Jesus to say, "I am the bread of life and if you come to me you'll never be hungry." But just what sort of work is required from us to make such an approach?

The people in the crowd give us a model to follow. They begin by not being able to find Jesus, looking for him in the wrong places. Then they have lots of questions for him that he refuses to answer directly; instead he challenges their motives for asking. It's about as straightforward as a conversation between the partners in a coalition government. And it gets worse. The people persist in asking Jesus to be someone he isn't and to make God turn religion into magic that gives us what we want on our terms. They quote tradition to strengthen their case: "This is what God used to do."

"No, it isn't," replies Jesus. "You've got your history wrong."

Finally the crowd stops arguing and starts listening. "Sir, give us this bread that gives life to the world."

Have they got the message? Can they see that the source of life and hope they hunger for is standing in front of them, present in the ordinary, day-by-day evidence of feeding and healing and supporting that's been going on all round them, led by this carpenter's son from Galilee and his fishermen followers? This is the slow work of faith that comes when you stand alongside people who need you, when you persist with your questions though no answers come, when you abandon the self-righteous feeling that you deserve better.

There is one prayer I try to say every day, even if I say nothing else at all. It goes like this:

> Help me find the way of love today,
> Open me up when I close down,
> Give me courage when I hold back,
> And sight when I can't see
> your presence and your leading.

It sounds easy but it's as hard for us as it was for the Christians John was addressing. They were caught in loyalty to an older synagogue tradition in which God supplied only one brand of bread, the one their ancestors ate.

Faith is work, the hard work of waiting, hoping, trusting, staying open to the grace that surrounds us, being willing to look for spiritual nourishment in all sorts of surprising places. We don't have to go a monastery on a mountaintop to find it. We don't have to look for neon signs and wonders to be sure about it. It's available in the midst of all the confusion of this crowd who went looking in the wrong place, asked all the wrong questions, for all the wrong reasons, misheard the answers, muddled up their own history. They were as greedy and stupid and misinformed as any group of people before or since, yet they still managed to end by asking for the life-giving bread.

We only have to ask, and trust, and keep at it. Believing is hard work, says Jesus. Believe me.

Flesh and blood

In a dispute with Jewish leaders, Jesus tells them that he is the living bread that brings eternal life, and through his own flesh and blood, he offers communion with God. (John 6:51-58)

If you're lucky enough to have such memories, think back on the holidays you might have had in warm places. Sun-soaked places. Smog-free places. By a beach, perhaps, or a lake. Under a summer blue sky. If you can remember such places, you might find that you left part of yourself behind there. I left my heart in San Francisco, goes the song, or on the beach at Waikiki.

Relationships with people have the same effect. To risk getting involved with someone else is to risk losing part of your self; leaving part of yourself with them, in them. The risk in any relationship is that you'll never be the same again. You might emerge shakier or stronger, but you'll never be the same. You probably know that already, if you've ever been in love, or bound in friendship or kinship of any sort. And if you've ever fallen out of love, if any sort of close relationship has broken down, you'll know that without any doubt. If you've been around for a while, you may still carry the pain that comes, not only from losing a lover or a friend, but also from losing that part of yourself you left behind in them. For some of us, the loss is so great that we never quite recover.

A huge part of our Western culture is devoted to pretending this isn't true. Pain-free relationships, fault-free dissolution of marriage are promoted like easy mortgages and insurances. Ring a number and someone will solve your problem. We can get away with this illusion of no-cost loving for a while but it collapses when we get down to flesh and blood.

Take blood donors, for example. They're desperately needed. We should all give blood. But an unspoken and primitive hesitation about letting go of something so precious confuses what is a simple, straightforward procedure. The example of kidney donors is even more powerful. The extraordinary stories we hear about relatives and friends offering one of their own kidneys to prolong the life of someone they love leaves us marvelling at their grace and courage.

Why does Anzac Day, New Zealand's annual memorial for its war dead, linger so powerfully in the nation's psyche? Why does its fascination grow among younger people, even as those who remember the war grow fewer? Surely it's to do with the flesh-and-blood sacrifice of those thousands of men and women. With twenty-twenty hindsight we can argue over how or even whether the wars they fought should have been waged. But for all our cleverness after the event, the lost lives and the wounds of those who survived speak with an unmistakable eloquence.

What did it cost? We ask that question of any relationship, any cause, any great adventure. If the answer comes back, an arm and a leg, we sit up and take notice. And when the answer is a life, flesh and blood, then we listen and we tremble.

Now it shouldn't have to be that way. If we lived in a world that was properly designed, audited by an international accounting firm and monitored by a good firm of management consultants, then we could surely have relationships that didn't bleed, we could create change that didn't hurt and we could build communities where no one became alienated and angry and wounded. We really could love each other without pain.

That's the kind of world we ought to have, but it's not the kind of world we've got.

Relationships cost us, and the deeper the relationship, the greater the cost. Now suppose that God is like this too, that in order to be close to us, God takes the risk of being vulnerable, just as we must do in order to be close to each other. And just suppose, when that happens, some part of God's own being is left inside each of us, and some part of each of us is left inside God, for ever. Just suppose that every time anyone suffers from giving or losing themselves, God suffers too, that God is immersed in every lover, every parent, every friend who gives and receives pain. And if God made a world where that is allowed to happen, God will share that hurt and absorb that pain. If that is true then the question becomes, not how could God do this to me, but why does God do this to Godself?

The claim the gospel makes is outrageous: the text seems to be saying, not simply that God loves as we do, but also that we need to let God love us like that in order to be fully alive. "Very truly I tell you, unless you eat the flesh of the Son of Man and drink his blood, you have no life in you... the one who eats this bread will live for ever."

Just suppose that might be true, next time you make your way up to the communion table.

Grace abounds

The author of this late-first-century letter to the Ephesians sets the place of the Christian in a cosmic frame, adopted as God's children, endowed with a glorious inheritance among the saints, saved by grace and raised to new life in Christ Jesus. All of this, says the writer, is a free gift from God, not of our own doing, nor the result of any works we might have done. We are, quite simply, what God has made us. (Eph. 2:1-10)

How you got anything to be thankful and hopeful about? I don't mean hopeful in an every-day-things-are-getting-better-and-better sort of way, even as the bank is bouncing your cheques and the hospital says your latest tests look awful. I'm talking about the hope and the gratitude you feel when you look the real world full in the face and find that tomorrow is still worth living for, when you meet people who are generous and brave and funny and strong when they have no reason to be, when you're humbled by people who are grateful just for life and breath and health and the colours of an autumn day.

I trust you have a taste of that hope and gratitude from time to time. I find it in the most surprising places, and it rarely comes straightforwardly; there are always compromises. But I'm glad that I even see some encouraging signs of hope in recent movies I've seen, even cynical films like Graham Greene's *The End of the Affair* where, despite all the obsession and the despair, a distraught lover and a betrayed husband who should have hated each other end up supporting each other in a moment of grace.

Funnily enough, none of my examples are conspicuously religious ones, but then I see as much evidence of wholeness and healing, liberation and life outside the religious community as I do inside it. And we're on strong theological ground when we see things this way, because the God at the heart of it all chose to be known through our humanity, in the midst of our history. Incarnation is the word for it. As John's gospel puts it, God so loved the world that God saved it. It's not the church that's being saved, not the religious folk, be they Christian or Jew. It's the world, lock, stock and smoking barrel, in all its mess and brokenness and beauty.

If you look only at the church, the signs of hope are some-times hard to see. If you widen the lens, then there is always something to be hopeful and grateful about. And we can claim that because we are confident that God looks at the world through a much wider lens than anything we can imag-ine.

But not everyone shares that confidence. Christians are increasingly divided over how God works in the world, and as churches grow more embattled and marginalized, set against the world instead of loving the world as God does, so an old heresy revives. It goes like this: there are really two worlds, a good one where God operates, and a bad one that's gone to the devil. The signs of hope, at the movies, in poli-tics and the environment, and among non-Christian people, have little or nothing to do with the salvation that God promises in Jesus Christ. They are all secular diversions from the sacred territory that religious people control. It sounds crude and it is. But overstated? No way. The heresy is called dualism. It's been lurking around the church since it began – John's gospel picks up more than a whiff of it along the way. And it's as alive and well today as it ever was.

The epistle to the Ephesians attacks this heresy, which claims for religious people privileged access to God's favour. The author explodes as nonsense the idea that those who toe the line will be guaranteed salvation. And he doesn't even try to soften the blow.

"For by grace you have been saved through faith, and this is not your own doing – it's the gift of God. It's not the result of anything you've done, so no one has anything to boast about." The logic of the passage is as sharp and clear as a snow-fed river. It goes like this: the evidence of God's life that we see in Jesus Christ is found in human generosity, joy, peace, forgiveness, patience, self-giving love. It comes like a gift, and even if we fight it, reject it, trample it, fail to recog-nize it, that gift is offered over and over again, to insiders and outsiders alike. But it's a gift we can never take for granted, even if we're sure we've received it. We can never possess it for ourselves or control it for others. As D.T. Niles once said, sharing the Christian life is like one beggar telling another beggar where to find a scrap of bread.

It's very hard to talk about those who are saved and those who aren't, because the boundaries are so hard for us to see. The angle of our lens is never wide enough. Even those who know how to say "Lord, Lord" have no guarantees of access to the kingdom of heaven, says Jesus. And you can't use measures like church attendance, otherwise all the clergy would be saints, or how much money you give away, otherwise multinational corporations would be sanctified.

In a post-modern, evolving, constantly restructuring society, absolute divisions between saved and unsaved become harder and harder to sell. It might be better to talk of ourselves as caught up in the process of becoming Christian, being saved as we travel further down the road of faith towards a future we can trust but not yet see. Think of our search for salvation as a piece of jazz, improvising, adapting as we listen to the other players, not relying on a set score, trusting that the melody will take us on, knowing it is a melody that God leads and loves.

For the letter to the Ephesians, the outsider was a Gentile Christian, one who hadn't had the proper Jewish religious background. You used to be "aliens from the commonwealth of Israel", he says, somewhat condescendingly. In our day, the equally sharp distinction is between those who work within a Christian frame of meaning and language and belief and those who see themselves as beyond that, post-Christian. The issue is not so much whether people are spiritually curious or not – most are. Or even whether there is curiosity about and respect for God. The question that divides is the way we communicate with each other about the spirit that gives us life and makes us human. The old Christian vocabulary is being stretched to breaking point and a new one is slowly emerging, though not quickly enough for some.

We are living through a great tidal change in the history of faith. It's a very confusing time, especially for those of us who are finding that we haven't left footsteps clear enough for younger people to follow with confidence. But in the midst of the chaos the message first sent to the church in Ephesus is as strong as it ever was: "For my grace you have been saved, and this is not your own doing – it is the gift of God." That gift is as available as it ever was. Just as freely bestowed, it turns up in the most surprising places and people, just as it ever did. And we who are seen to be religious hold no more control over that gift than we ever did.

Thank God for that. Thank God for the generosity and the extravagance of grace that gives life and hope for ever to everyone who seeks such gifts.

PART TWO
Occasions of Grace

Christmas faces

Have you ever had the experience of hearing about someone you once knew, maybe from long ago, but not being able to recall the face? You may remember where they live, even know their name, but their face remains a mystery. Worst of all, you meet again someone you once knew, but fail to recognize them at first. It's very embarrassing, especially if it's an old girlfriend or boyfriend – the ultimate insult.

Ours is a bad era for violent crime. There are too many security camera pictures on television of faces hidden behind balaclavas. Too many pictures of men in prison garb with their faces blurred to avoid recognition. Too many hidden cameras trying to pin public faces on private stories. As a society we are desperate to find faces we can know and trust.

In order to be fully human, we need to put names and faces to the people and the forces that shape our lives. C.S. Lewis wrote a marvellous science fiction novel about that basic human need. He called it *Till We Have Faces*, a phrase borrowed from a Greek myth. "How can the gods meet us face to face till we ourselves have faces?" Lewis wrote. And to do that "you will be forced at last to utter the speech which has lain at the centre of your soul for years. A human being must become real before it can expect to receive any message from the superhuman: that is, it must be speaking with its own voice (not one of its borrowed voices), being for good or ill itself, not any mask or veil."

In the story of the birth at Bethlehem, God finds a face, a human face, a baby face.

Not the face of a warrior king. Not the face of a politician who can restructure the economy and get it right this time or protect the land from the military invasion. Not even the face of a magic supernatural miracle worker from above the clouds. Just a baby. Helpless like any other baby. Born to parents who were ordinary, tired, bewildered and not a little afraid. The baby's name is Jesus. The baby's face is God's.

But how can it be that God becomes helpless, dependent on our response? Does God take the risk of waiting for us to recognize who this baby is? Why doesn't God find a safer, clearer, proper grown-up way of being with us?

The mystery of Christmas will take the whole of the next year to unravel and we will still be left with a God whose way of loving confounds us completely. But we can make sure that we don't leave this story in Bethlehem. The face of God we find in this story is not limited by time or geography. Wherever, whenever a baby is born, we can recreate the story and find God's face again – the closer the better.

We also need a Christmas story in which we can find our own names and faces, whoever we are. In Bethlehem, they didn't limit the party to good church-goers who paid their mortgages on time and kept out of trouble with the law. The shepherds were a rough and smelly lot with a fondness for things that fell off the backs of trucks. The wise men were weird, foreign followers of strange religions and cultures.

There are no limits on who can stand around the Bethlehem manger, no good behaviour requirements, no membership qualifications. We can't say we're not good or worthy enough, or religious enough, or smart or fat or thin or good-looking enough. We can't even say that we don't believe enough. This baby with the face of God welcomes all comers.

If we can cope with a God who takes such a risk, this God can cope with us. If we dare to show our faces and say our names before this God, whoever we are, then we can glimpse the face of God. That's what this Bethlehem story, this face-to-face story, is all about.

Transfiguration now

The Australians may be good at rugby but they are better at television programmes, and one of my favourites is the police drama, *Blue Heelers*. In a recent episode the locals were coping with a miracle worker and the town priest, called in to advise the constabulary, told them, "For those who believe, no explanation is necessary. And for those who don't, no explanation is possible."

He could equally well have been speaking about the baffling story of transfiguration in chapter 9 of Luke's gospel where, in the presence of three terrified disciples on a mountaintop, Jesus is bathed in dazzling light and talks to Moses and Elijah. It's almost impossible to make sense of, any more than we can make sense of the music a choir sings only by reading the score. It baffles us because it relies on a leap into the unknown that our heart and soul let us make, even if our head says no. It's a leap that requires imagination more than intellect. What we're talking about here is the stuff that miracles are made of, the magic of transformation, the subject that bewitched the Greek novelist Nikos Kazantzakis, whose favourite three of God's creatures were "the worm that becomes a butterfly, the flying fish that leaps from sea to air in an effort to transcend its nature, and the silkworm that turns its entrails into silk".

So what help does the gospel story give us in decoding transfiguration so that we too might experience what Peter, James and John experienced as so terrifying, mystifying and life-transforming? The answer is, not much. But there is something to be going on with.

The transfiguration happens at a time of crisis. Jesus has just told his followers that they are going to end up losing their lives if they want to save them. The price tag on this new business of being Christian has just been set, and it's very expensive. This week I've been involved with a family of four children where both parents have lost their jobs, three people who have been greeted with the news of terminal illness, another who is facing long hospitalization, yet another who is experiencing financial ruin. They're all struggling to make sense of what's happening to them, struggling to understand what God is up to. And they are all candidates for transfiguration, transformation to a new level of experience, a new way of seeing the world. How that might happen, or whether they'll let it happen, is beyond me. But it's crisis time for them, as it was for Peter, James and John, however hopelessly ill-prepared they were.

We're told they heard what Jesus had said, eight days before, but there's no evidence that they understood anything. In fact, these three friends who climb the mountain with Jesus to pray are a dopey lot. In the midst of the amazing things that are going on, they have trouble staying awake, and when they eventually get a glimmer of what's happening, they suggest a wildly inappropriate response. Peter says they should build three dwellings to house in stone spiritual visions that can never be housed. Then we're told they're terrified, and finally, having been through this experience of a life-time, we learn they "kept silent and told no one any of the things they had seen".

What's the text saying? That in order to have life-changing spiritual experiences you need dopey friends who rush around wanting to do things immediately? Maybe the text is saying that God's transforming love and grace will work in you through your everyday relationships with the people closest to you, even if those people are not especially smart or religious or high-powered. Even if they're a bit sleepy or inclined to make the wrong decisions. Even if the puddle you share with them is very small.

Because this experience of transfiguration is not dependent on us. It always comes as a gift, as R.S. Thomas writes in this beautiful little poem, simply called *Gift*:

Some ask the world
and are diminished
in the receiving
of it. You gave me
only this small pool
that the more I drink
from, the more overflows
me with sourceless light.

That's transfiguration: the experience of sourceless light. When it happens it takes us, God's ever unready people, by surprise – dazzling us, terrifying us, leaving us lost for words.

The only comfort is that others have been through this before us, and proved equally ill-prepared. One of the good things about celebrating transfiguration in a cathedral like the one I work in is that we're surrounded by a great cloud of witnesses to the truth of God's transforming power in their lives: devout people who sat in the nave week by week, wonderful musicians who sang and played their hearts out, craftspeople, cleaners, stone-masons and artists who could see God in small things as well as in large structures. Many of these witnesses didn't believe much in any orthodox sense; you don't have to be able to chant the creed to testify to transfiguration. In their art and craft, in their daily occupation, they held out the hope and the promise and, once in a while, a passing glimpse of God's ability to bring light out of darkness, hope out of despair. As Emily Dickinson wrote,

Hope is the thing with feathers
That perches in the soul,
And sings the tune without the words,
And never stops at all.

Are we getting anywhere with this mysterious gift called transfiguration? Can you connect it with anything wonderful, beautiful, hopeful that has ever happened to you? Any experience where your life was opened up to see a wider country and a bigger sky and a further horizon?

I hope you've had a taste of something like that and that you're willing to let God be part of that, even if you didn't give him credit at the time, or know what name to call her.

But whether we have or haven't had such a taste is not really the bottom line for this story. Because it claims to be universal, true for all the world. The truth about the God we see in Jesus Christ, the generous promises of love and justice this God holds out to everyone, are there for all the world to see and enjoy, for anyone who chooses to seek life instead of death, in whatever form it takes. It doesn't depend on what we did or didn't feel last Sunday, or tried to define in this creed or that, by this church or the other. Let's not try to domesticate it or make it merely personal. It's a much bigger sort of transfiguration we're talking about here; the sort that transforms the world for good, good for everyone, good for ever.

With Jesus, in the company of friends, surrounded by those we love who have gone ahead of us to glory, we stand hopeful and expectant, holding out nothing but empty hands, not trying to control or dispense, but simply to receive, trusting that the gift will come, whether we're ready or not. Where it might take us, how it might change us, God knows.

Last ride down Main Street

Open any newspaper, switch to any television or radio channel, and you will very quickly be treated to a close encounter with a celebrity person of the exotic kind. It will be someone well known for being well-known, probably rich, perhaps good-looking, well used to talking, but not usually with anything very profound to say. I won't mention any of the names of people who annoy me intensely, even though their faces are always being thrust in my face. They stare up at me from the magazine racks in the supermarket, they lie in wait for me when I turn on the television, the news bulletins recite their silliest comments with reverence.

My dislike is not so much for what they've done; often their stories are interesting, especially when they've had to cope with failure, illness, hardship, parents who didn't love them, obesity or anorexia, and endless lessons from the school of hard knocks. What disturbs me is the stupendously excessive amount of time and space devoted to their stories and their faces. In some perverse way, the more trivial their message, the more attention they seem to get. Being wise or truthful or honest seems to have nothing to do with the amount of coverage they receive.

There must be a positive side to this obsession with the rich and the famous. Maybe it's our need for heroes. In a world where you can enjoy medical miracles immediately if you have enough insurance, where the world is your oyster if you know how to open the shell of your Internet and e-mail, we still need heroes to inspire and direct us. And the heroes we choose speak volumes about who we are. Some celebrities I encounter in print or on videotape leave me feeling slightly soiled for having met them; others enrich and uplift me. So the older I get, the fussier I am about the company I keep through books and movies and television programmes. We have a right to be choosy about our heroes, because they affect us more than we know.

The church faces a problem of marketing a hero. In most Western countries, our credibility has slipped so badly that most people no longer even think of Jesus as a hero. A good man perhaps, but goodness alone doesn't guarantee you heroism, any more than it does for a kind old uncle. A mysterious, somewhat obscure man, someone we don't know very much about – there's potential there, but it's a long way from captivating our attention.

The early church had no qualms at all about making Jesus into a hero of the sort that first-century people could recognize and admire. It wasn't a matter of inventing a story to make him heroic; they simply rearranged the story of what did happen to make it engaging. Each of the gospels does that in different ways, for different audiences – some more Jewish, some more Gentile and Greek – but the hero mould is evident everywhere, especially for the Greek audiences.

The classical hero formula is clear: born of a virgin or some equally unusual circumstance like a celestial light, precociously talented as a child, trapped in an inescapable destiny of greatness, suffering innocently, choosing to die with honour at an early age (heroes don't grow old or fade gently, they rage into the night), tempted by divine enemies yet challenging them and overcoming. From Achilles to Agamemnon, the formula is followed with variations, almost always by a man who is courageous, just, balanced and humble, never above himself or guilty of self-pride. These heroes can be classified as humans adopted by gods, or born as children of gods, or angels in between humans and gods, or gods themselves. Christian theology covers all its bets with explanations about Jesus that echo all four of these categories, and they're laid out in detail by theologian and classical scholar Gregory Riley.

Of course Jesus isn't defined or captured by any of these explanations or formulae, but they did shape how he was first presented by the early church. The first Christians were confronted with a figure who showed them more about God than anyone ever had before, even the heroes in their own sacred history. The conventions of the classical hero worked for them, serving to introduce Jesus to millions of people who hadn't heard of Moses or Abraham or Adam and Eve.

But do they work for us, in countries far from the Middle East, at the beginning of a new millennium? Clearly not, in

Aotearoa New Zealand at least, otherwise we wouldn't be the least churched, most secular society in the Western world, and we wouldn't have to put up with the silly stereotypes of Christianity that are bandied about in our media.

We need urgently to recast the Jesus story so that it resonates with the land and the culture where we live and move and have our being. We need a Jesus who sings our songs and wears our clothes, eats our food and talks our talk. A Jesus who we can imagine in our midst when we share a meal together in a café, when we stand around the bedside of someone we love whose illness makes no sense. We need a Jesus who speaks our language, who wins the admiration of the youngest as well as the oldest in our midst, the poorest as well as the richest. We need a Jesus who can be a hero for each of us, before he can be a saviour for any of us. Only then can he do the job he came to do, which is to point us towards the mystery of love and the promise of life eternal.

It shouldn't be too hard. We have all the raw material we need and nowhere more abundantly, with more contemporary connections, than in the Palm Sunday story. For here we have a hero who makes his last ride down Main Street. Gary Cooper couldn't have done it with more style. Here we have a hero who has avoided self-importance to the point of swearing his followers to secrecy about who he is, but now for one last bright morning, knowing that the celebrations will very soon end in crucifixion, he indulges the crowd who want to honour him with a parade that any victorious sports team would feel flattered by.

This is a story soaked in courage and tragedy. It mixes jubilation and devastation. There are crowd scenes and a lonely hero on his way to die. There's a cast of characters, faithful friends, who do everything they're told, even as they prepare to betray their leader and run away.

This is a story about a hero who is more than a hero. It deserves to be the subject of every talk show, every feature page, every television special. It won't be, because the media prefer more trivial subjects and the church has lost its nerve and has settled for protecting a hero who needs no protection, who only needs our imagination and our courage to live his story for him, on his behalf, in the strength of his spirit.

There is no better point of entry into the Jesus story than this Palm Sunday procession. There is no easier way of joining the crowd, in the front row shouting aloud, or quietly in the background, watching the hero ride by, deciding whether we dare to follow.

Seeing ain't believing

Growing up, I was very conscious of the presence of my grandfather in my grandmother's house where I spent a lot of time. I could picture him striding up the street where he worked and where I rode on my bike. But I had never seen him. He died long before I was born.

From the war books I devoured as a child, and black and white movies like *Angels One Five* and *Reach for the Sky*, I was vividly aware of the power and beauty of the Merlin-powered Spitfire and I could draw the symmetrical sweep of its wings and tailplane with the greatest of ease. But I'd never seen a real Spitfire.

I'd never seen a cathedral of any size until I went to Christchurch as a university student, but I was utterly familiar with the soul-satisfying lift of a Gothic arch and the grandeur of buildings designed for queens to be crowned in and bishops to be buried in. I knew about cathedrals because I'd seen them in newsreels at the picture theatre and photographs in magazines – bombed and restored, or miraculously spared in Europe.

You don't have to see to believe. Not first-hand. Second-, third- and fourth- hand are okay. Indirectly and roundabout are okay. Passed through a generation or two so the story can be smoothed and shaped a little. That's okay.

If you're lucky enough to have known your grandfather or seen a Spitfire or grown up with cathedrals, then I'm envious of you, of course, but I don't know if I'm worse off. The stories I've gathered about the things I love but haven't seen, the play I've made with my imagination, the testimonies I've heard from others about these things and the richness of the heritage that now enfolds them – all this means I can believe without seeing, just as vividly as the closest eye-witness.

There are some very crude caricatures of the Easter story that would have you believe Jesus sat up suddenly one morning, shrugged off all the horror of the week before like a bad dream and got on with the job, enjoying the added power of walking through walls and finally ascending to heaven, preferably on a cloud.

It's all very amusing but it doesn't have much to do with the New Testament accounts of what happened. In Luke's version there isn't even a body. There's no sign of anyone resembling Jesus. Only a couple of angels who scared the early morning daylights out of the women who came to the tomb. No habeas corpus here, only words that the men dismissed as idle tales, women's gossip. The men know what to trust. All Luke gives us to go on is the absence of a body that was last seen three days before – and the absence of a body can mean bad news as well as good.

Absence isn't much to go on. The other gospels aren't much more help to us if seeing is believing. Matthew's later version of the story has Jesus appear briefly after the angels but the earliest account in Mark has no sign of Jesus, only a single angel saying you're looking in the wrong place. And in one of the two alternative endings to Mark's gospel there are no resurrection appearances at all. In John, Mary mistakes the man who appears to her for the gardener.

There are later appearances on the beach, in the upper room, on the Emmaus road, but the Easter morning stories that make the greatest impact on our imagination and our faith are surprisingly light on direct evidence of Jesus rising from the dead. And even if there were more first-hand accounts of Jesus sitting up and walking out of the tomb, they wouldn't help us get to grips with this Easter story, 2000 years later.

What's at stake here is not simply what happens to Jesus but to all of us. There is no tag on this story to apply it only to good, or even not-so-good, Christians. It's a universal story available to anyone who lives and dies and wonders what it's all about. The breathtaking audacity of the Easter message is that God challenges death in all its forms, for all its victims. We will still be crucified and we will still all die but that will not be the end of the matter. God will not fix us up, but God will transform us. This is not about some new sort of therapy. It's about eternity, and we can enter it again this morning if we choose to.

Easter is the invitation to let our living and our dying be caught up in the eternal life of God – a life that will transform us and exalt us as it did to Jesus Christ. The beauty and the mystery of that defies any words, which is why we resort to music like Schubert's Mass in G, and if you don't understand the Latin words, it doesn't matter a jot, because none of the words do justice to the miracle of what happens on Easter morning as Christ is risen and so are we. Down the centuries faithful people have let their lives be transformed by the Easter story and, surrounded by that cloud of witnesses, we dare to say with them that Christ is risen, and so are we.

Are you ready to say that? The disciples weren't. The women were prepared to deal with death, not life. They came with spices, expecting to work on a corpse. What's more, they had forgotten where Jesus had told them to look for him. And the men weren't prepared for anything, it seems, not even to deal with death, let alone new life. They stayed home, crying in their beer and dismissing the women's story as an "idle tale". You couldn't have found a more poorly prepared lot if you tried. It's Resurrection Day, and the world's worst reception committee lines up to announce it, then collapses in terror and amazement, falling over each other in panic and confusion. What a story! So much for the advantage of being on the spot with first-hand evidence.

We often worry in our churches and our ecumenical gatherings that we haven't enough money or the right people or the know-how to make this gospel story understood. We sometimes despair that this Easter promise of new life reaches so few of the people who need it most. And some of us long to be clearer and more certain about our faith. If only we could be confident. If only we could touch and see for sure.

The Easter morning story tells us to stop worrying; to revel in the freedom we have to believe without seeing; to have faith without having to be sure; to walk the road without having the distance measured and the destination clear; to trust the support of other travellers who have walked ahead of us and who walk with us now.

Easter is a stand-up story

I asked a seven-year-old friend of mine to tell me what he thought about Easter. "It's okay," he replied, "but I'd rather have Christmas. The food and the presents are better."

For many church people Easter is okay but it's Christmas that draws the crowds because there's more to celebrate, more to connect with. You can't beat the marketing appeal of a baby's birth, let alone a holy baby's birth. We endlessly expand the symbolism of Christmas, so that the hopes and fears of all the years are born in us again.

But doing that with Easter, letting that resurrection story on that first morning become our story, is much harder, especially if the menu for the season isn't exciting. The Russian Orthodox Church knows better and cooks up the finest, richest recipes for Easter Day: cakes with two dozen eggs. Many of us have to settle for roast dinners and chocolate eggs wrapped in foil.

In a strange way, Good Friday is easier to market than Easter. Death, like birth, is straightforward. It happens to the best and worst of us. Three of the four top movies in a recent line-up for Hollywood's Oscar awards were about wholesale death and dying on battlefields and in concentration camps. Although we hate to admit it, death has real entertainment appeal. Television ratings go up when there's a war to watch.

But Easter eludes many of us as a festival to make our own. Why is it so hard to share the fear and terror of those first disciples and taste the exhilaration of what they experienced?

If what they found was really true, then it is still really true now. If what they found had a use-by label and faded after fifty or five hundred years, if resurrection isn't as good for the third millennium as it was for the first, then it's not worth celebrating anyway. We should hand it over to the historians for safe-keeping.

Easter is so easy to pick up by the wrong handle. It's a story that modern readers can listen to and then, so easily, lose the plot. For example, we can treat it as a story about resuscitation rather than resurrection, as though Jesus came back to life just he was and went on with his work, pretty much as he did before. The internal evidence for that isn't strong because the risen Christ is not even recognized at first by some of his closest friends, but you can force that "magical" meaning on the story.

The other extreme is to make the story purely spiritual and deny the physical reality of any sort of bodily resurrection. This would go down well in a New-Age context where spirituality is fashionable as long as it stays other-worldly, and a metre or so above the ground. But this is a story about a ghost that eats and drinks, that walks on dusty roads and cooks breakfast on the beach.

We are well trained to separate the spiritual and the physical, body and soul. That dualism is still our modern disease. The Easter Christ offers an integration we can't easily accept, so we go chasing other ways of understanding the story. For example, maybe it's all to do with us, all our fault. We don't appreciate Easter because we don't believe enough. We're the problem, "O we of little faith". We don't come to church enough, we can't recite the creed, we can't make sense of it all. So Easter is a story for the really religious. The rest of us mark time and hurry on to Christmas.

Woody Allen would make a good movie out of such introspection, but it doesn't fit well with the Easter texts. The four gospel accounts are full of people rushing about in high states of personal anxiety, shouting out that they don't know what's going on here, that they can't see and they don't understand. The early church didn't like such discomfort any more than we do. The history of the church is a headlong rush to pin down the faith in formulas that everyone could memorize and understand. But we're cursed (or is it blessed) with this Easter story of uncertain witnesses, bewildered disciples, told in several versions.

Mary Magdalene herself offers two refrains: "They have taken him away and I don't know where they have laid him" and then, even more powerfully, the line that has haunted everyone ever since who has tried to follow Jesus, "She saw Jesus standing there, but she did not know it was Jesus." Imagine what people struggling to survive might do with those words, people we know who are crushed by the weight of personal tragedy or illness or disability, or people stripped of their human dignity by poverty or violence or abuse of any kind. How could these people even expect to see Jesus standing with them at all?

That's not surprising because, like us, Mary wasn't expecting to find him in the middle of uncertainty and confusion. If she expected anything, she expected to find a corpse which, after all, is what many people expect to find in the body of Christ today. Dead. Serene and composed, of course. Secure. No surprises. Lying down. Instead, she found someone standing up and, once she had coped with the shock of that, she herself and all the other disciples stood up too and the church as we know it got onto its feet.

So what's all this standing up got to do with resurrection? Nothing, until you look closely at what the word resurrection really means. And, like so many translations of Greek words into English, it sells us short. The New Testament uses two different words, one means to wake or rouse, the other literally means to rise to one's feet, to stand up. The English word "uprising" picks up some of the force of this meaning, but it's usually limited to political contexts. Resurrection, then, is all about that energy that lifts us to our feet when we're falling over, that lets us stand up and stand tall when we're weighed down. It applies equally to individual lives and to whole communities.

And the experience of resurrection doesn't have to wait until all is well and everything is clear and all our relationships are on course. It first happened in an early morning of great confusion. It goes on happening to us in the midst of our brokenness and our pain. For some strange reason, resurrection is clearer in the aftermath of some sort of crucifixion.

And it certainly doesn't depend on how religious we are. One of John Grisham's best-sellers, *Testament*, on the face of it has nothing to do with resurrection. The central character, Nate O'Reilly, is a failed father, lover, lawyer, a drunk and a tax evader. He's sent off on one last assignment to Brazil where he's involved in a plane crash, a riverboat disaster and another drinking binge. But despite all that he manages to start to turn his life around: "He was stiff and sore from the plane wreck and still shaky from the vodka of the night before, yet Nate pulled himself up and stood unaided in the centre of the deck, wobbly and bent at the knees. But he was able to stand and this alone meant everything. Recovery was nothing but a series of small steps until he could stand."

Closer to home, I had a visit from a friend with serious addiction problems whom I hadn't seen for months. "I've come to tell you", he said, "that I've met Jesus. He was standing right there beside me, telling me to get up and turn my life around. And I am. Next week I start a long treatment programme." Now I've heard lots of people tell me they've met Jesus and I make up my own mind about their claim. The issue isn't whether they get the name right. It's whether they stand tall as a result of that meeting: that's the measure of resurrection. And there's no doubt in my mind about my friend on that score. However resurrection comes to you, it is still part of the same Easter morning experience whereby God's renewing love and energy lifts us up and lets us stand tall. And, in the process, we become a sign of new life, God's life.

Signs of death are all around us. We have no trouble recognizing them. But signs of resurrection are harder to see because we aren't sure what to look for, what to expect; it's almost too much to hope for. The Easter gospel is saying, don't make it too complicated. Settle for signs of people and families and communities who are standing up, getting on their feet again. Trust those signs to point to a God whose energy and love can lift us up, whoever we are and however and wherever we fall.

Nobody saw the resurrection, whatever it was, happen on that first Easter morning. The guards at the tomb came closest but they slept through it all, we're told. But what people did see – the woman Mary first, then women and men ever since – is someone standing up, and inspiring and empowering others to rise and stand tall, even if we're not able to explain quite how that happens. "She saw Jesus standing there, but she did not know it was Jesus." Do we dare to expect to see him standing among us now?

New life now and then

What comes to your mind when you think of resurrection? New life that follows some kind of death? New hope that follows some sort of despair? You've heard the phrase "a new lease on life". What experiences does that trigger for you? For me, all sorts of very recent happenings come to mind.

Immediately I think of people I know who have been through a rough time, emotionally or physically, and somehow, despite the odds, often with a courage that leaves me speechless, pick up their lives, rejoin the community and offer energy for other people's wellbeing. I think of people I know fighting their way out of the black pit of depression, or the paralyzing grief of losing a loved partner, or coming to terms with disability. I meet such people all the time, and they leave me feeling overwhelmed by grace.

I think, too, of some of the movies I've seen recently. You could equally well think of concerts you've been to or books you've read or art works you've seen – anything that represents new life from someone else's experience and makes it transparent and accessible to us. The films I'm thinking of tell the stories of an old man's journey on a ride-on mower to make peace with his dying brother, or a young man's return to the orphanage of his childhood to pick up the work of a doctor who performed abortions on the side, or a boxer's impossible struggle to break a sentence for murder with the help of an illiterate youngster. They all sound like the stuff of soap opera and some are. But they weave the threads of new life and new hope and redemption through the dross of the ordinary and the mundane. And, as such, they are the stuff of Easter theology for the thousands of people who prefer a cinema seat to a church pew.

All these are the experiences that frame for me the gospel story of the first Easter morning, from which I draw the confidence to even imagine the possibility of new life and new hope. The details of the gospel story remind us of the terror and confusion and surprise that new life can create when it comes out of unexpected times and places and faces. But it's all couched in language and images designed for the early church to understand.

They knew how amazing it was for women to be witnesses to something so important, or how familiar and proper it was to have angels floating about, or how important it was for their hero Simon Peter to have a role. The story worked for them because it connected with images and memories and cultural practices that were still familiar. They were able very readily to connect their vivid experiences of new life and new hope with the Easter morning narrative. It was written for them, on the assumption that they would know what was being talked about.

And it's written for us, on the same assumption. It doesn't stand alone. If we can't fit this Easter morning story into the frame of experiencing some form of resurrection now, then it quickly becomes a rather bizarre account of resuscitated corpses and early morning confusion. For resurrection then to make any sense, it needs to be connected to resurrection now.

Wait a minute, say the doubters. Resurrection now is a messy business. Your examples are all ambiguous and open to argument. Let's keep it clear and simple and stick to the old, old story. Nice thought, but the old story is just as ambiguous as our new one, just as filtered through history and culture and prejudice. Do you really think the first disciples saw it all clearly at the time? Don't forget that the story we're reading was written down much later. Ambiguity was as troublesome for them as it is for us.

Aha, say the cynics, this "then-and-now" connection works only for insiders. It's an internal Christian argument you're having with yourselves, and it makes not a scrap of difference to the way the world works.

Oh dear, say the Christians, isn't resurrection our word, something that happens only in the hearts of true believers?

None of these voices is taking the Bible very seriously. Let's look at some texts. John's gospel begins with the outrageous claim that, in the beginning, all things came into being through the Word or the activity of God. You can state that in the present and future tense as well as the past. Without God, nothing happens. God is the one in whom we live and move and have our being, the source of all life and every experience of life being renewed, restored to fullness; every such experience is an experience of God.

And if that doesn't raise the stakes high enough for you and dissolve every distinction between resurrection then and resurrection now, try Paul's letters. God in Christ is before and in all things, and holding all things together, even the whole creation which is groaning towards fulfilment as a woman in labour. And when we don't know how to put all this into words and pray as we ought, the Spirit of God does it for us, with sighs too deep for words.

It's all there in the scripture – in those few sentences I've compressed a dozen texts – spanning then and now, church and world, Christians and all God's people, bound by a vision that overarches everything we do, undermining all our neat distinctions between who deserves to know resurrection and who doesn't. On Good Friday, we say this prayer: "Let the whole world see and know that things which were cast down are being raised up, and things which had grown old are being made new, and all things are being brought to their perfection."

That happens on Easter morning, if we dare to let the connection be made between resurrection then and now. If we talk only of resurrection now, real though it might be for us, from this moment on, next time we walk on the beach, or fall in love, or see a great movie, we'll cut ourselves off from the source of energy for all new life, and we'll risk missing the best way of ensuring we don't sell this gift short and cheap, reducing it to a feel-good experience, an Easter morning that skips past Good Friday.

If we talk only of resurrection now, we'll only know it now and then. But if we make the connection between this morning and that first Easter morning, resurrection will become our daily expectation, built into the way we see the world and trust the future to unfold.

New life now, as then, no matter what's happened, no matter who we are. That is our birthright by baptism. That is the promise of Easter morning.

Angels and dinner parties

I don't get the feeling all that often, but there are times of the year when I'd like to see an angel. It wouldn't have to be a very big one, or for very long, but I'd love to have a glimpse of one at Easter time. I never have, and I envy those who enjoy what Luke's gospel calls a "vision of angels", which is how the two disciples describe what the women saw on Easter morning. The disciples sound just a little envious as well, I'm happy to say.

I'm not after the angels of the flaky, television kind, which tend to dominate European experience. And that might be my problem: I'm living in the wrong culture. In Mexico and Spain and the Balkan countries, I'm told, they see angels all the time – often in the form of women who look like Mary. And there are countless stories of monks and nuns who pray and wait and pray some more and do see angels.

I don't have that kind of patience but I do respect those who wait on angels. And my respect rises at Easter time. Because as I read the resurrection stories again, I'm surprised at how dependent they are on angels. In all four gospel accounts, one or several angels of various sorts are the first ones to break the news. And in one of the versions, the angels are the only ones to tell the story. The risen Christ doesn't appear in person at all.

The overwhelming balance of evidence of resurrection in the New Testament stories is through indirect means: other people's accounts, stories passed on and retold, visionary experiences of angel-like messengers, often in dreams, hints and glimpses of a Christ who is somehow present but somehow different from the way they knew him before Good Friday. But very, very few people have the privilege of a first-hand, full-on encounter with an angel, let alone the risen Christ. And among those who do, there is a high percentage of psychiatric illness, which makes it all the harder to sift the truth from the illusion.

Last week, on a religious television channel, I watched a Hollywood actress talking about Jesus. Jesus told me this and Jesus told me that, she said. He told me to go here and park there and phone this number. I don't want to deny the sincerity of this woman's faith, but I do want to argue that that sort of direct-dial, in-your-face kind of experience of God is not the only kind the Bible describes. And in Luke's Emmaus road story, I believe another way of encountering God is being offered.

It's a very elusive, indirect and quite mysterious kind of meeting that the two disciples experience on the road to Emmaus. They set off on a 10-kilometre walk and are joined by a stranger, a man they don't recognize, who talks with them, very knowledgeably. In fact he challenges them for their lack of faith and understanding, and still they don't know who they're talking to. Then he leaves them but they urge him to stay and eat with them.

It's not until they start to share the meal that they recognize him, and the minute they do, he vanishes.

It's a great story because it will be very familiar to many of you who have struggled to understand what it means to meet the risen Christ and walk with him, without the benefit of angelic interventions. And the two disciples will be familiar too. They weren't among the favoured ones at the Last Supper, they probably didn't witness the crucifixion and they certainly didn't see the events of Easter morning. All they had to go on was the women's story about visions of angels. They didn't bother to go and check out the empty tomb for themselves. These are cautious disciples, two or three steps removed from the story. Good people, no doubt, but not wanting to get too involved. They'd make good Anglicans.

Now we could feel sorry for these disciples, just as we can feel sorry for ourselves, those of us who haven't encountered angels, let alone the risen Christ. But that would be to miss the point of this story and the amazing gift it offers. It promises that you can meet the risen Christ in a new way that is as personal and immediate and real as if you'd bumped into him physically.

And that new way is a meal, as simple or as fancy as you like to make it, anywhere you'd like to have it, any place, any time, with anyone, in which the bread is broken and the wine is poured, the food is blessed and shared in the name of Jesus Christ.

That's all? Yes, that's about it. Wherever two or three are gathered in my name, there I will be in your midst. And the bread, it's my body given for you. And the wine, it's my blood poured out for you. Do this to remember me.

The remembering here means more than musing over a memory. It means recalling the story in a way that recreates it, re-enacts it. The meal is indissolubly mixed with the story of how it happened – rooted in the Jewish Passover tradition, the radical practice of open table that Jesus practised, the risks he took at including all comers, even those who were to betray him, the notion of meal as hospitality and service. This meal was laced with memories of dusty feet being washed by the host, expensive oil being poured on his hair and all sorts of strange companions – Jewish leaders slipping in after dark to avoid being seen, foreigners from out of town, disciples who talked too much, tourists who watched and listened and went on their way. This is a meal immersed in a noisy, messy story of all kinds of people with nothing in common except a curiosity about the host and why it is that anyone who eats with him gets a glimpse, if they're watching, into the very heart of God.

So how do you meet the risen Christ, the resurrected one? Wait for an angel? That's always an option, and if it happens, rejoice. But in the meantime, sit down to a meal together. Whether you like the other diners or even know them is irrelevant. Gather together what's available, give thanks for it and for each other. Retell the story. Make peace around the table. Ask for a blessing on what you do. Share what you have. And Christ will be in your midst.

Should it be in a church? It doesn't hurt. Do you need a priest? Well, that's good for connecting the meal with the story and the tradition that nourishes it. Should all the guests be baptized? Well, that certainly underlines where the meal belongs.

But none of those things define the presence or absence of Christ. They're only attempts by the church to make it clear why we eat and drink like this. The church's job is only to make the meal accessible to new people, to ensure that the hospitality of our altar tables reflects the hospitality of God.

The trouble is, it's all too simple. How could the living presence of the God we know in Jesus Christ be entrusted to something as ordinary as a meal of bread and wine? Don't ask me how, but it is. And until I run into a vision of angels, I'm going to trust that meal as the best evidence I know of resurrection.

Christ is risen. He is risen indeed. Pass the bread, share the cup. Eat up. Drink up.

Christ is risen indeed.

Getting a handle
on resurrection

Great music. Classic hymns. Lovely flowers. Hot cross buns for morning tea. My Lord, what a morning. We sing and act on Easter morning as though everyone present in church is perfectly clear about what we mean by resurrection. Christ is risen. Indeed. Indeed he is. But of, say, a hundred people gathered in a church for the Easter celebration, I would bet that you could find a hundred different understandings of resurrection.

If that's even halfway true, then some people will be very upset – the self-appointed guardians of orthodoxy who tell us what we should believe, or not believe, about this Easter story. On the one side there are the heavies who insist that every detail of the biblical record must be literally true, all four versions of the story, even though each gospel tells it differently. And at the other extreme, we have the equally dogmatic advocates of the line that it's all a fairy story and nothing really real happened on Easter morning. God is dead.

My Lord, how boring. If God is dead then it is boring because there's nothing for Jesus to get up for this morning. Nothing for us either. Because Easter is finally a story about what God is like, and whether he or she really is the "giver of life". Reduce Easter to a nice idea about a dead God of either gender and we stay stuck back in Good Friday or Saturday, locked in a time warp of despair. I'd prefer to stick with the confusion and excitement of a hundred different understandings of the story. Because I think that's what the Bible is offering us, depending on who's telling the story and who's listening.

If you have recently lost someone you love then you'll hear this story differently from someone whose life is rolling along sweetly. If you favour a woman's version of a story over a man's, if you have trouble with angels or insist that seeing is believing and hold that someone else's story can never be trusted, then you'll interpret this Easter story in radically different ways. And the beauty of what we have on offer is that there's room for all those differences, and a hundred more. That's how rich and wide and deep the resurrection record is.

It's based on four gospel versions with as many different threads as there are common patterns. Jesus is dead in a garden tomb. There are women visitors in the pre-dawn dark, but the numbers and names vary. The tomb is open, but for different reasons. There are angel messengers but what sort and how many? Several answers are offered. There are military guards in some versions, but not in others. Sometimes they fall over and faint – very unsoldierly behaviour. Sometimes they get bribed to spread rumours. In one version only, there's an earthquake. In another, a gardener appears who turns out to be Jesus.

In all the stories, everyone is very confused, running about in the dark. Strong words are used: terrified, dumbstruck, confused. In all the versions, the men have trouble believing the women.

Does all this make the story any less believable? No, it increases its reality. Try to remember any traumatic event you've lived through. There are bound to be a dozen versions, sincerely held but not quite agreeing, from all those involved. If we can treat these differences as bonuses rather than liabilities, food for celebration rather than suspicion, then we can start to use them as handles to hold on to so we can grasp what resurrection is all about.

Because for modern, science-driven, secular minds it's such a hard story to get inside. Take it at face value and its outrageous, impossible, magical, unbelievable. Many people treat the Easter story like a roadworks sign that says "sorry for the inconvenience", when in fact the clear intention is to delay the traffic for hours on end. But the story isn't designed to be read and believed like a road sign. It's all about a group of people who knew far more about Jesus than we ever can, who loved him to death, and were suddenly faced with having to know him all over again in a new way. And they coped by grabbing hold of a variety of different handles.

Some of them had a first-hand encounter not with Jesus but with angelic messengers of various sorts.

Some of them met a Jesus figure but didn't recognize him, and when they did, hours later, found that he'd changed.

Most of them met no one themselves but relied on the testimony of people they trusted.

Some of them believed on the basis of absence not presence. An empty tomb was enough. Or even a stone door that had been inexplicably rolled aside. Some of them remembered what Jesus had said months, even years before, predicting the manner of his death, and put two and two together.

Some of them believed by sifting through all the evidence, discounting the rumours, looking at the changes in the lives of other disciples. Some of them didn't look too hard at what was happening in the present but focused on the future, expecting that somehow God would be with them in the Christ after Good Friday, as God had been with them before. They tried to take seriously the advice of the angels: look for someone who goes ahead of us.

Those are just a few of the handles that the gospel stories offer directly. There are dozens more that we're not told about and have to discover between the lines. Imagine what the people involved in the story – guards, gardeners, early morning workers in the city – who saw something of all this confusion and shouting would have said when they went home to their families that night. "You'll never believe what I ran into this morning down by the cemetery."

Time and again, the bystanders in the Christian story get caught up in the action. It's a dangerous story to hang around because it can involve you before you know it. The church is full of people who came to faith reluctantly, without meaning to – by having a conversation with someone who impressed them, by finding that a moment in their life coincided with a symbol or a song or a word that spun them out of themselves and into the mystery of God.

Which brings me to the final handle on resurrection that the gospels offer us: the option of losing control over the story and giving up any attempt to make sense of it. Think about it. The people who eventually believed most passionately in the risen Christ began in utter confusion and terror, running around in the dark. They didn't know what to think.

None of it made any sense. Far from managing the story, they had to let the story manage them and give themselves over to wherever it might lead.

This kind of surrender is scary stuff but it's a prerequisite to finding out what resurrection might be all about in your life. You can grab onto all the handles you like, and there are plenty to choose from, you can listen to the eye-witnesses, and weigh the evidence and recall the biblical promises, but finally you have to give yourself over to the story.

Unless we take that risk we may well find ourselves stuck in Saturday, or wallowing in the misery of Good Friday, never quite able to own the excitement of Easter Sunday morning. But if you can take the risk, and let the confusion of this story wash over you and in you and through you, then the experience of resurrection, new life out of death, hope out of despair, will start to well up and pour out – in relationships you'd given up on, in the challenges you'd found too hard till now, in the pieces of your life that had fallen apart and now just might come together again, after all.

When that happens, and it does, then all the arguments about whether Jesus really broke the bonds of death back then, and exactly how it happened, look slightly silly. If he didn't then, how can we even begin to talk about resurrection now? As we can, as we do on Easter morning. Christ is risen. He is risen indeed.

Imagine a church that made sense

Whatever else the Pentecost story is about, it's certainly about the birthday of the church. Jesus had been getting people ready for this church for a long time, with mixed results. It looked for a while as if no one in Israel was listening and nothing was going to happen. But on this day, it all begins in Jerusalem, among devout Jews from all over the known world, who are suddenly able to communicate as never before. So it's certainly a birthday story, but it's more than that, and that's where the trouble starts.

Is it also a slam-bang story, a close encounter of the religious kind, that knocks you off your feet? A sort of first-century pentecostal experience, a Toronto Blessing? Because if that's the case we should expect another one, at least every birthday: wait for the violent wind and the divided tongues of fire flickering down and the instant languages. If that were true, then nothing much has happened in the church for a long time. Most churches don't have such experiences regularly.

Something incredible happened on that Pentecost day in Jerusalem. The Jews who came to the festival to mark fifty days from Passover got more than they bargained for, but this is a piece of theology before it is a piece of journalism, and we need to read it as such to get beyond the superficially miraculous.

You can't even class it as a straightforward offer of ecstasy. What is experienced here is not the speaking in tongues that Paul later describes as the least of the Spirit's gifts; those tongues you can't understand without another inspiration to interpret them. These Pentecost tongues are languages that make sense, across all the cultures.

To a good Jew, the tongues of fire would have immediately connected with the pillars of fire that guided the people of Israel by night through the wilderness. Others listening would remember the fire that is promised in the baptism Jesus brings. I baptize with water, says John, but Jesus baptizes with fire. And the reference to wind would have linked with dozens of Old Testament passages that show God speaking through a voice that is sometimes a violent, sometimes a still and small voice. For wind was experienced as the breath of God, that same breath that blew across the face of the waters on the first day of creation.

As for the countries in the catalogue of visitors from out of town, this was no casual list of holiday destinations: it mapped the boundaries of the known world. If you went beyond Egypt, Asia or Mesopotamia, you fell off the edge. These people who gathered in Jerusalem represented the whole world.

And what about the long passage that Peter misquotes from the prophet Joel? A good student would have picked up the mistakes, because Peter changes the tense of the passage several times to show it's all happening now. The last days have arrived. The Spirit God long promised for our sons and daughters is being poured out today.

So what is this story about? Why is it being told today? How has it assumed such huge importance that the church marks its birthday by it?

Far from being an invitation to await another miracle, the story makes more sense if we read it as a blueprint for the mission of the church. Treat it as a carefully assembled demonstration model being given a first test drive in Jerusalem in the hope that all the world will buy it, and the story starts to make a lot of sense.

What does it say? If you want the Holy Spirit to show us what sort of church we're meant to be, then gather together in one place, and wait. Listen, watch, pray, be expectant and be available. If we're anxious about ourselves and our own importance; if we're preoccupied with being properly recognized and rewarded, or trying to hang on to the past at all costs, then we're probably not available to the Spirit. We're probably getting in the way.

At the general synods of the Anglican church in Aotearoa New Zealand and Polynesia, time and again we face the problem of one *tikanga* (cultural pathway) being in too much of a hurry; not able to listen and wait to hear what another is saying. The breakthroughs have come, not when the cost accountants prove their case or the lawyers amend an amendment, but rather when voices once ignored are finally heard, offers of hospitality are made and accepted, old injustices are recognized at last. In a culturally complex church of women and men, European, Maori and Polynesian, the Spirit requires of us plenty of time to watch and wait and listen. Otherwise we might well miss the Spirit when it comes. What's more, we need to be open and expectant as we wait – ready, willing and available.

And if we're ready and willing, just what does this Spirit do? The usual way of answering that question in today's church is to talk about feelings and special experiences of the kind that makes good television footage. That might be part of the story; as New Zealand poet James K. Baxter says:

Lord, Holy Spirit,
You blow like the wind in a thousand paddocks,
Inside and outside the fences,
You blow where you wish to blow.

But that's not the point of the story of the first Pentecost. Whether we enjoy special experiences or not, the Spirit enables us to make sense of each other, to understand and be understood. It is the Spirit that allows the church to become comprehensible, not simply to itself, but to the outside, making Christianity comprehensible to our sons and daughters, letting what happens inside churches have some impact on what happens right out on the edges of our known world, among whoever our neighbouring Parthians and Medes and Elamites might be.

And who might they be? The trade union we don't support? The gay and lesbian community? The immigrants? The political party we aren't going to vote for? The people who like the music we love to hate? Whoever, for us, is outside, foreign, beyond our understanding, those are the people that the Holy Spirit enables us to communicate with, if we let it.

Bishop John Taylor wrote the best book of his life about the Holy Spirit. It's called *The Go-between God*, that part of God that connects us one with another, especially when we don't want to be connected because we're afraid, dispirited, inadequate, shut down. It's the Spirit that gives us the confidence, the hope, the imagination and the nerve to open up, not only alone but together, for everyone, in every culture.

Thinking about this Pentecost story, I wandered through the lunchtime crowds in the central city, trying to imagine what might happen if we let the Spirit work as I believe this story intends. Imagine if people really did expect the church to be a place of acceptance and inspiration, justice and love; if they comprehended that this gospel we talk about each Sunday belonged equally to all of them. Imagine if this gospel made as much sense to young as old, in Japanese as in English, in pop song as in plainsong, to the broken and the angry as it does to whole and happy people.

Imagine a church that did make sense to all those people who don't come near the church. Could we cope?

Let's take the (od)d out of God

It's very hard to find a text about the Trinity. Matthew's Father, Son and Holy Spirit baptismal formula is the only text in the Bible that comes close to mentioning the Trinity by implication, though if you had asked anyone at the time what the Trinity was, they wouldn't have known what you were talking about. It took another two hundred years before the word was used. Our English word comes from the Latin, which came from the Greek, from people who were speaking Aramaic.

But Matthew's story does mention the three-in-oneness of God, whereas the other three versions of the same story don't. In Mark there is no mandate from the mountaintop in Galilee for trinitarian baptism across the world; instead it's a dinner-table promise of miraculous signs. In Luke, Jesus blesses the disciples in Bethany; they leave immediately and go to church. In John, Jesus appears in Galilee but not on a mountain and all the focus is on Peter.

Four very different ways to answer the question, what is God really like and what does God really expect of us? Convert the world? Wait for miracles? Go to church? Follow the leader?

For the next two hundred years, the church didn't have much time for speculation about all this. The first Christians were swamped by the speed with which their church grew, the anger of their opponents and the confusion of their cross-cultural spread across the known world. It took a Roman lawyer called Tertullian in the late second century to find the time to sit down and write out how all these different ways of talking about God might fit together. Things had got into a bit of a muddle and then, as now, lawyers were eager to take on impossible tasks.

How can God be above it all yet also in the middle of it all? How can an immaterial Spirit be reconciled with a very material human being with his feet very much on the ground? How can God be universal and all in all, yet at the same time have a special interest in Jerusalem, or your home town, for that matter? How can the creator of pain be the bearer of pain? How can the giver of our life allow us to destroy our life?

The church had to do something about this mess because it was tearing itself apart with heresies that played off one understanding of God against another. A new language was needed to unravel the jumble. On offer was the Greek vocabulary of theatre and neo-Platonic philosophy that talked about persons, literally *personae* which could be faces or even masks, characters that could be assumed. Tertullian latched on to that idea, translated the words into Latin, making them more about people than the roles people play, and the idea eventually arrived in English and gave birth to the hymn that says: "God in three Persons, blessed Trinity".

Three persons? One, two, three. The old prayer book reinforces that separation when it asks us to believe in three persons in one God, each with separate seasons. So we meet God the Spirit at Pentecost and God the Son at Christmas time. The potential for confusion is huge.

When this person-centred doctrine of Trinity hit the twentieth century, obsessed with personal psychology and individual self-development, any hope of containing that subdivision of God disappeared. If you want to see the worst excesses of God's captivity in personal psychology, watch the American televangelist programmes in which the hosts sit on brocade couches in Armani suits chatting about the three personalities of God as though he, never she, is a buddy at the ballgame. I found Jesus: he was hiding behind the sofa all the time.

It's true that God invites us into intimate, passionate relationships. It's true we can fall in love with God. It is personal. But that is not to say that God is a person as Bob and Carol, Ted and Alice are. And nor is God able to be separated as Bob and Carol, Ted and Alice are. That's not what the doctrine of the Trinity intended. Our problem at the beginning of the millennium is that it's very hard to free it from person language.

We need a church that is at least as bold in the twenty-first century as it was in the third and fourth, a church that is confident and skilled enough to take responsibility for describing God in language that the people of the day can understand. You can't leave that to the Bible, because the Bible doesn't talk about the Trinity. This supremely important attempt to say what God is like is left to the church. We draw on the experience of the people of God, the story of God's Spirit at work across the world and through the early church, the life and times of the Son of God. All that is most reliably recorded in scripture. But we're still left with the question that the disciples said out loud on the day of Pentecost: What does it all mean? How does it all fit together? The church wrote that question down, thought about it for three hundred years and answered it with the doctrine of the Trinity, using the best vocabulary of the day.

What is the best vocabulary for our day? How can we now stop God being subdivided into competing personalities, separate people? How can we stop the farce of Christians telling each other, "I know God better than you because I've met his Spirit, well I've met her spirit, well I know the Son personally, well I'm a friend of the Father." If we really want to make sure no one new comes to church, then let's go on talking to each other like that. We could simply hold onto the old language about God, male, monarchical and separatist though some of it is, do what we can to correct it, batten down the theological hatches and hold on tight. If you worship in a traditional church, you're going to have to live with some of that old language anyway because it's built into the music and the architecture, to say nothing about the piety and the personality of some people.

But we could also temper that old language with new images to honour the fact that a relationship with a living God requires a vocabulary that is being constantly expanded and renewed. If you're in love with someone and forty years later you're still talking about him or her in the same way you did on your first date, then it's probably time to do a little linguistic renovation.

We've got plenty of help with that task of expanding our description of a triune God, lots of new sources of imagery and metaphor – in fact they are mostly rediscovered from earlier forgotten corners of our tradition – that talk of God in organic terms as fire, water, wind, brother moon and sister sun; in relationship terms as father, mother, lover, friend; in travelling terms as companion on a journey; in biological terms as breath, life, healing energy; in the language of music and art and quantum physics and astronomy; in the language of silence and contemplation.

The sky is quite literally the limit when it comes to expanding the way we talk and conceive of God, so long as we honour the wholeness and the oneness of God, the endless unconditional depth of God's love and grace; the endlessly renewing, interconnecting, communicating, go-between dynamic of God; the universality of God, the accessibility of God; the unqualified welcome we each enjoy into the very heart of God.

That's what the doctrine of the Trinity ought to be saying to us and, even more importantly, to others who are listening at our doorway. It ought to be saying that this God talk is normal, natural, healthy, open, ordinary, everyday stuff. And if it isn't then let's sing and talk to each other until it does. That's what being church is all about. Let's take the odd out of God.

Falling glory, rising doubt

Believe it or not, an FCRT is a foliage accumulation reconnaissance technician, employed by the council of the city where I live. Every autumn he prowls the shady streets, checking out the leaves, following up the phone calls that come into the control room of the city streets unit. The FCRT is a kind of undercover hired gun, armed only with a cell-phone and a leaf-blower. He's out there for us, facing down trouble before trouble shoots in the form of flooded drains and blocked pipes. This man for one season deploys the teams of leaf-rakers and suction engines who gather up the once glorious foliage and cart it off to be recycled into a garden fertilizer called Envy.

Envy indeed. I'd love a job like that. He probably gets to drive one of those little tractors, which must be even more fun than a ride-on mower, he travels the city, meets grateful people who probably bake him fresh pastries and cakes. Being an FCRT sounds like a great job.

Best of all, the FCRT gets to see the best of the city's autumn displays, those last, shorter, still days before the cold winds come, when the trees are draped in reds and golds, yellows, oranges and browns that defy a painter's palette, so saturated are they, so radiant in their beauty and their warmth. Then the wind comes, and overnight they're gone for ever, leaving stark, bare branches that promise only a cold winter without colour. It happens so quickly. The final spurt of autumn has come and gone before you know it. The greatest beauty lasts the shortest time. The FCRT would see that more sharply than most of us. Maybe it wouldn't be such a great job after all...

Easter time is the season that promises us new life and new hope, but people complain every year that it's silly to celebrate Easter in the southern hemisphere when everything in nature is dying off. I'm not convinced we've got the timing wrong. In the northern hemisphere, it's easy to believe in resurrection when spring is breaking out all around you. No wonder Europe is full of green gods and maypoles and folk religions of one sort or another.

At our end of the world, you have to work much harder to trust the promise of new life and hope in a dying season, when all the evidence of nature is working against you. The last splash of autumn beauty makes it all the harder, all the more tantalizing as the beauty intensifies before it fades and dies. But once the leaves have gone we struggle to find some signs to steer by through the winter months. It's hard to get excited about the promise of Easter when the cold weather is rolling in and your house isn't well heated, or your health is shaky or your job is being restructured again or your children say they plan to stay home till they're thirty, or your relatives say they'd like to come and stay for a month or two and you don't have a spare room. At least a springtime Easter suggests that something's going right in the world. Autumn leaves offer no such reassurance. You've got to face what's happening to you without any natural assistance from the season.

The challenge of celebrating Easter in Aotearoa New Zealand is the challenge of daring to expect new life and new hope against the grain, from dismal days and unlikely events.

It's tough, but not as tough as it was for Michael Lapsley, a New Zealand priest who gave his life to the anti-apartheid struggle. In 1990, living in exile after being banned from South Africa, he received a parcel in the post that turned out, on opening, to be a bomb. It destroyed both his hands and one eye but it didn't destroy his spirit. If anything, it's stronger than ever. Today he heads a centre for healing and recovery from trauma in South Africa, travels widely and speaks confidently, and with an indisputable personal authority, about turning loss into redemption. He talks of his ministry with people who have lost everything in the struggle to end apartheid and yet manage with the help of the community of healing he has formed to find enough hope to keep living. They even learn to laugh and sing again. People like Michael Lapsley teach us that even in the winter of our deepest discontent and our greatest despair, after every autumn leaf has fallen and every sign of hope has gone for good, new life can still come if we expect it to.

Recently I went to the funeral of a man who'd lain in silence for five long winter years, completely disabled by a stroke. He'd spent his best years as an armourer with the Royal New Zealand Air Force, excelling with his great commitment, his love for life, his passionate care for his family, his overflowing energy and generosity. During the service, his younger son read a poem for his father, all about flying through the clouds, climbing higher and higher, reaching up to the sunlight to touch the face of God. The memories shared during that funeral made that a wonderful metaphor of a life richly lived, a spirit that a ravaged body and a hard, slow death could not contain. Somehow, the experience of new life filled the small church on that autumn afternoon. Resurrection happens, even when we don't expect it.

But whether we expect it or not, there are some things to help it along. A community of people, for a start. Someone to talk to, someone to listen, if only to say out loud that the leaves have gone and you'd like some help to rake the lawn. A willingness to accept that change is inevitable, ongoing, inescapable and we must welcome it, go with it. And a confidence that new life will come, no matter what. A confidence that there is another way, even a better way, when the road in front of you runs out. A trust that even the rubbish dumped in your life can be recycled into something that will be the envy of others.

This promise is not something that we wait for passively, as we wait for springtime, without having to do anything about it. The expectancy we're called to hold on to is a habit of the heart that goes against the flow of a pessimistic society preoccupied with dying rather than living, swayed by appearances, settling for quick fixes and easy solutions, ready to give up hope when the first leaves fall.

The Easter promise is made of tougher stuff. It knows all about the last glory of falling leaves. Palm Sunday is the symbol of the short-lived triumph that precedes the tragedy, the sunshine before the storm. Good Friday is the eye of the storm, where the worst that we can inflict on each other is carried by one who deserved it least. And Easter Sunday is the promise that no matter how impossible the odds are against you enjoying new life, it does still come, it can still happen. Death doesn't have the last word.

Of course the promise of new life is harder to see and hold on to. It turns up unexpectedly in bomb blasts and funerals. Often we can see it only through a glass darkly, very rarely face to face. We have to look hard to find new life under a pile of autumn leaves. New life is harder to find than dying life; it rarely comes painlessly or naturally. What's more, it will disturb us when we do find it, when it does come, because it will change us for ever. But come it will, especially if we dare to expect it in the autumn – there's no better time to look out for it.

The facts of heaven

Springtime is driven by flower power. Yes, it also means longer, warmer days. People are in a better mood. Colours are brighter. That's all true. But it's the flowers, especially the daffodils, that have the last word about spring.

Personally, I'd rather have a hot pie than a daffodil. I'd rather go to the movies than walk in the park. And I don't really believe that those daffodils all pop up out of the ground spontaneously without any help. I think there's a secret army of gardeners that work through the winter months, under the cover of darkness, wearing black balaclava hats, spreading fertilizer and injecting hormones into the underground bulbs, to help them make their springtime debut in a riot of yellow blooms.

And it is a debut, a first appearance, though we've seen the daffodils arrive so often year by year. It ought to feel like a re-run, a simple repetition of the same old colours and the same old shapes at the same old time. Yet somehow it isn't. In some mysterious way we experience as if for the first time, just as we do a new day. Morning has broken, like the first morning. Daffodils too.

Just as the return of these flowers takes us by surprise, so does their message. Even though you can communicate faster by sending an e-mail, flowers still speak louder and say more, even when there are no adequate words to be found. One of the abiding images of the nightmare in East Timor was the flowers piled up in the cemetery at Dili, or, in a tragedy on a much smaller scale, the mountains of flowers that filled London in the week Princess Diana died. Flowers send a multitude of messages, and none more vivid than the ones that Jesus employs, when he uses the flowers at his feet to help us stop worrying about the future. Consider the lilies, he says. They don't do a scrap of work to justify themselves or secure their future. They don't feel anxious or guilty about anything. And yet they flourish.

It's a message we've been slow to receive. Ours is a time obsessed with performance appraisals and endless reviews. We have to justify everything we do, provide cost benefit analysis, double check accreditation. Listening to what the

flowers might be saying to us in the real world is like looking for little green men or talking to plants: you're liable to
be ranked as certifiably insane. So in these post-modern,
post-enlightenment, new-millennium times when we think
we know so much, we start on the back foot if we try to listen to what the spring flowers might be saying to us. And as
for decoding what William Blake is saying – "To see a world
in a grain of sand,/And a heaven in a wild flower" – well,
what are you talking about?

We've lost the art of listening to things. It takes us all our
time to listen to people. And as for expecting a thing, like a
flower, to give us a glimpse of God, well, I ask you. Get off
the grass.

We might get somewhere if you asked us to see God in
the way we behave. For ours has been a moralistic heritage,
fixated on good behaviour, following the rules, keeping on
the straight and narrow. Our popular wisdom is full of
images of lives kept clean and tidy, decent and in order, managed by the principles of good housekeeping. Our Western
individualistic culture honours those who don't get into trouble, don't cause a nuisance to others, obey the road code,
keep their heads down and their noses clean. A thousand
funeral eulogies sing the praise of those who died good as
those who go straight to God.

I think, however, that this way of seeing the world is
slowly being replaced by another way: more individual,
more subjective, less consistent, less manageable. This new
way is centred on how you feel. What's true and what's good
depends on your emotional response to the people around
you. And if you're up or if you're down, then the whole
world goes with you. This new way doesn't talk directly
about God much, though it is profoundly spiritual. But when
it does go religious it goes with a hiss and a roar and God is
met with great intensity and passion. Hearts don't just get
strangely warmed. They're superheated. They boil over.

There is, though, another way of encountering God, a
very old way, that we've lost sight of today. It's a way of seeing the world that was around when Jesus told his parables

and, much later, when William Blake's poems were written. Without it, we will never experience the truth they told with anything like the same vividness and power. And we will never be able to listen to all that the spring flowers might be saying to us.

It's a very simple way. All it takes is a trust that the simplest things have the power to speak, in their own right and for their own sake, simply because they are part of God's good creation. Glory be to God for dappled things, wrote Gerard Manley Hopkins. He may as well have added, and for plain or coloured, odd-sized or ordinary, small things or extra large, underwater or extra-terrestrial things, mass-produced or home-grown things, glory be to God. Because everything has the capacity to speak of God, to give honour to God. That's not an invitation to worship things, for that would be idolatry. You don't even need to kiss rocks or hug trees. It's nothing more than a challenge to trust that heaven really might be found in a wild flower, that ordinary things can point us to the heart of God.

This ancient way of seeing the world has come and gone like the wind throughout Christian history. The Eastern church understood it better than the West, the Celts grasped it better than the Romans, the Irish often better than the English, women mostly better than men, jazz musicians better than... well, never mind, comparisons are odious.

Wouldn't it be good if we could manage in the new millennium to spend less time worrying about the way things ought to be and the way people ought to behave and feel, and more time valuing and celebrating things as they are, letting them say what they have to say, and taking the time that might require.

We could start now by listening to what springtime says to us, next time it rolls around. Trust the things of spring to speak to you, let them become what they are created to be – channels of abounding grace and confidence in a future we can trust.